AN ANGEL IS BORN

An Angel is Born

A Family's Story

Wynn Johnson

AMBER SKYE
PUBLISHING

ISBN: 978-0-9894003-0-5

Library of Congress Catalog Number: 2013908575

Printed in the United States of America

First Printing: June 2013

17 16 15 14 13   5 4 3 2 1

Edited by Angela Wiechmann
Designed by Mayfly Design and typeset in Arno Pro

AMBER SKYE
PUBLISHING

1935 Berkshire Drive
Eagan, Minnesota 55122
651.452.0463
www.AmberSkyePublishing.com

To order, visit www.ItascaBooks.com or call 1-800-901-3480.
Reseller discounts available.

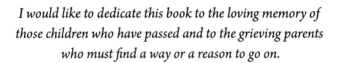

I would like to dedicate this book to the loving memory of those children who have passed and to the grieving parents who must find a way or a reason to go on.

CONTENTS

PREFACE

Every family has its rebels, its quiet ones, its smart ones—and its mediocre ones, such as myself, who swagger through with a C+ average in life's overall accomplishments. There are also those who stand out and succeed without apparent effort. There are always family members who teach us, lead us, and organize us.

However, when a family member comes along with the ability to change us without saying a word, to listen but not criticize, and to love unconditionally and touch us so deeply, then it's worth the effort to write about that individual.

I'm writing this book about three people who are very dear to me: my sister Lily; her husband, Bill; and their daughter, Angel Rose. My girlfriend, Jessica, and I were sitting in our backyard at our home in Plymouth, Minnesota, a Minneapolis suburb, when she turned to me and said, "This is a story that has to be told." That was about a week and a half after Angel Rose's passing. It's a love story like no other, she said to me. It was decided then and there. With her help and Lily and Bill to guide me, the project got underway.

• • • •

The first part of this book takes a look at the history that shaped Bill, Lily, and Angel. One doesn't just wake up one day and become an exceptional person. I'm sure you'll agree we're shaped by not just our parents, our teachers, or our loved ones, but by all the above, along with every event that happens to us, good or bad, from the cradle to the grave. So in order for the reader to understand Lily and Bill, I find it necessary to describe the times, people, places, and events that made them who they are today.

There are lots of short stories within this book, especially in the history section. The stories are about the lives—and the deaths—of a number of people very close to us as friends, neighbors, or kin through blood or marriage. The stories are true, and the people are real. None of the names have been changed, and I have made every effort to tell these events in the most accurate and truthful manner possible. If anyone reads this book and finds cause to be offended for any reason, then I hope he or she will be good enough to forgive me. It is certainly not my intention to offend anyone in any way whatsoever.

Many things have changed in the more than six decades outlined here. Some things were good and some not so good, but for those of us who lived it, a look back is nostalgic to say the least.

• • • •

Most of the book is, of course, about Bill and Lily as well as Angel's life and then her death. The most foreboding thought that can haunt a parent is that of losing a child. Some children are taken by tragedy, while others suffer long and painful illnesses before succumbing to fate. As my mother said when my brother passed away in October 2000, "Parents are not supposed to outlive their children. It's just not supposed to be that way." This statement couldn't be more true. However, as tragic as it is, it happens. There's no way for a parent to prepare for the death of a child. It is always untimely, unexpected, and merciless.

Other tragedies often follow when a child is lost. Divorce, drug or alcohol abuse, insanity, and even suicide are often the result of losing a child. There's only one known antidote, and that is faith in life everlasting. Faith in a reunion at a place of health, happiness, and eternal tranquility. That is the only concept that keeps most parents on a steady path to recovery.

Bill, Lily, and Angel's story is not just about the death of a child. It's also about the life of a child so special to all of those around her. Angel's story is unlike any other, but yet I know there are many cases when children such as Angel are born with birth defects and require special care throughout their lifetimes. There are many stories of heroic parents such as Lily and Bill who transform their entire lifestyle and everything around them in order to keep their children alive. But there are other parents who are unable to provide for their children with special needs and have to retire them to nursing facilities. Sadly, it almost always means a shorter life for the child.

I realize it is both physically and mentally demanding to care for a child who is handicapped. In many cases, it involves around-the-clock care, and the task becomes greater as parents age beyond their ability to care for their children. In addition to this is the enormous cost for medical care. As we all know, children with special needs are not always born to the privileged or to families with exceptional healthcare plans. We also know that money and insurance plans are not always enough to ensure the well-being of a child with disabilities. Case in point would be Rosemary Kennedy, sister of the late president, who was eventually placed in a home in Wisconsin.

The fact is, there's no substitute for the genuine love and care of parents—parents with sometimes nothing more than faith in prayer to sustain them as they lose sleep, worry, work laboriously, and cherish each and every moment of their child's existence with little hope in sight. It is, however, an insult to imply to these parents that caring for their child is a burden. To them, it's no different than when you care for your child who is suffering from a severe cold or flu. Do you simply go to bed while your child is coughing or has a fever? I'm sure we all know the answer to that.

One thing I've learned from speaking to parents of children with special needs is their feeling of being alone. They feel isolated from other family members. It's human nature to shy away or distance oneself from the suffering of others. Even with the love we all share, we all secretly find ourselves avoiding others' suffering. I believe this is one cause for the feeling of isolation all these parents share.

And sometimes, despite the family's assurances of love and support, the parents still feel alone in an arduous and never-ending struggle. It often adds to the loneliness when friends or family members unknowingly make comments such as, "I don't know how you do it" or "You're not going to be able to do this forever, you know."

All these parents share an unexplainable characteristic: they possess an unusual strength that drives them beyond the abilities of ordinary people. It's a self-imposed will to go the distance and learn what it takes, and it's the willpower to use that strength, even if the odds are against them. It can be nothing more than divine faith.

His way is perfect; The promise of the LORD proves true;
He is a shield for all those who take refuge in Him.
                                                    —2 SAMUEL 22:31

INTRODUCTION

The tombstone reads: *Mom, Dad, and Jason. A team always.* Those words, along with a photograph, can be found in a cemetery in Dayton, Minnesota. It's a small but beautiful cemetery located on a hill overlooking the Mississippi River. From the mid-1990s through the early 2000s, we lived just across the road from the cemetery, where we would often stroll on Sunday afternoons. I continued to visit Jason's grave, although I'm not really sure just why. The picture was of a young boy, about fourteen, with his parents, who looked to be in their midthirties.

I don't know the circumstances of Jason's death. I only know that in the picture, Jason appeared to be completely healthy. I came to believe he had been the victim of a tragic accident. I would stand by Jason's graveside for a few moments, shake my head, and wonder how Jason's parents could find the strength to go on. I would then secretly give thanks for having two children who were—and still are—alive and healthy. A troubling thought would then come over me. An almost audible voice would say to me, "This can happen to any family at any time." I realized how easy it must have been for fate to rip Jason from the grasp of loving parents.

Parents are everything to a child: mentors, doctors, providers, protectors. It begins at birth and continues as the child matures.

"My tummy hurts, but my mommy will be home soon, and she'll make it all better."

"My dad's not afraid of those monsters. He'll chase them right out of that closet. He'll find them, even if they hide under the bed." "Guess what? My mom's teaching me to drive. She says that if I continue to do well in school, they'll buy me a car after I graduate."

But this is a progression many parents are not allowed to enjoy. When fate intervenes, it is remorseless, it has no memories, and it pays no homage. It is a helpless feeling for any parent when their child is sick. The only thing that could possibly be worse is not being able to do anything about it.

A child is made of two physical parts: one part mother, and one part father. When parents lose a child, they also lose those physical parts of themselves. Needless to say, the suffering is much greater than if they had lost limbs. When one loses a limb, there is hope in the skill of the surgeon or the aid of mechanical devices. None of this hope can be found when the death of a child occurs. So what can parents do when all seems lost? I truly wish I knew.

• • • •

An Angel Is Born is a story of solemn truth, never-ending love, and poignant sorrow. From the beginning of mankind, angels have descended to earth to interact with humans. There are far too many stories to be ignored or dismissed as myth. In fact, there've been so many accounts of angels that we have titles for them, or rank and file. There are cherubs and seraphim.

I want to tell the story of an angel who was born to this earth in the flesh. Her name is Angela Rose Skiles. She was born at Community Hospital of Springfield, Ohio, on the second day of May 1972. It was in that building that Angel took her first breath, and it was in that same building that she took her last. Angel lost her struggle for life on October 1, 2011.

Angel was born with numerous defects that tormented her for nearly four decades. This is not to say Angel didn't enjoy life. She loved to play, she listened to music and watched TV, she laughed and she loved.

Many things make Angel's story unique. She never displayed one moment of anger or the rebellion parents often experience while raising children. Angel was and is still, somewhere beyond the sunset, an angel. Angela Rose Skiles, Angel, is my sister's daughter, and we miss her sorely.

This is her story.

Precious in the sight of the Lord is the death of his saints.
—PSALMS 116:15

PART ONE

History

Chapter One

This story begins in Appalachia. There is a universal and stereotypical opinion of Appalachia from those who've never been there. They've learned about Appalachia only from TV or movies. But I would like to share with you some things perhaps you didn't know. This will help you understand how such remarkable people as Bill and Lily Skiles can be products of Appalachia.

Seasons are evenly balanced in the eastern Kentucky region. It's hot when it should be and cold when winter comes. Spring and autumn are mild and temperate. There is such a large variety of wildflowers and blossoming trees in the spring, and if you've never seen that part of the country in the fall, then there's just no way to describe the beauty or the colors. Mid-October is the peak season for viewing the foliage. This is when the lower canopy has dropped enough leaves to color the ground, while the brilliant colors of the upper canopy contrast against an azure sky.

Many species of trees are found in the Appalachian region, but oak, hickory, and poplar stretch upward for more than ten stories. Wildlife consists of woodchucks, raccoons, squirrels, and rabbits. Larger animals such as coyotes and mule deer are here, and black bears were extinct in the area until recently but have been reintroduced and are now thriving. There've also been unofficial reports of mountain lions. There are reptiles as well, some harmless while others quite venomous.

The wet season lasts from late autumn through mid-spring. Streams flow from the mountainsides, carrying rich topsoil to the lowlands below. This creates excellent conditions for vegetable and flower gardens. Morning glory, honeysuckle, and other vining plants grow thick and lush on fences and trellises. The sound of the frogs in early March is a welcome prelude to spring. New leaves begin to appear in mid-April, and the apple, cherry, and peach trees bloom as well. By early summer, they'll be heavily laden with fruit.

Warm spring days are filled with the sound of the robin, the brown thrush, and the goldfinch. At night, the song of the whip-poor-will can be heard from dusk until dawn.

Summer days can be hot and humid, but when the heat becomes too much to ignore, folks head to the mountaintop which always offers a cool breeze and panoramic scenery. The mountaintop is easily accessible by pickup truck or all-terrain vehicles via the coal trails.

Weeksbury, Kentucky, is in the heart of Appalachia and along the western edge of the Cumberland Plateau. It is, to say the least, off the beaten path, with the closest main highway about fifteen to twenty miles away. However, that's the way people of that area like it. They don't mind the extra drive time to work; because they know when they get home, they're out of the rush and the hurry. People of all ages gather on weekends to camp, picnic, and listen to music. Dick Bartley's oldies can be heard on Saturday night, but it's an area deeply seated in the country and bluegrass heritage.

Folks there do indeed love visitors. Endearing friendships are formed when strangers come to visit. Everyone is welcome— but you better come prepared to camp or stay with friends, because the closest motel is about thirty miles away at Pikeville or Prestonsburg.

Route 466 is the only way in or out of Weeksbury. Near the entrance, the road splits. The road to the right enters a hollow, or a canyon, called Number One. The road to the left leads through a different hollow called Caleb Fork. These names were given by the geological surveyors who first discovered coal in the area. Railroads were built deep into these two canyons as coal mines were opened along both sides of the mountain. Communities formed in both canyons, and a school was built in the Caleb canyon. This created a merger between the two communities that formed Weeksbury. At the junction of what would become the Caleb Fork and the Number One roads, there was a theater, a post office, a general store, a soda fountain, and an office building—all of which were owned and operated by the coal company. It's important to mention that Number One extends north from the split as Caleb continues to the west. Both hollows have short or smaller hollows that branch from them like fingers or tree roots. At the western end of Caleb Fork, Shop Hollow turns to the south for about a half mile.

• • • •

Coal is still the pervading industry, although mining techniques have changed a great deal. Workers still go underground, but strip mining is the most common method for extracting coal. Blasting and massive machines are used to remove large portions of the mountain to expose the coal. Environmental damage is horrendous, but it's an ugly fact we all must live with until alternative energy sources are found.

The industrial boom reached the eastern Kentucky mountains just after the turn of the twentieth century. Coal companies built railroads to the headwaters of every creek or river. They brought in large amounts of manpower and equipment and built machine shops to service the equipment.

The primeval forest was leveled to provide lumber to build houses, stores, and shops—all of which were owned by the coal companies. They gave miners credit to buy whatever was needed to make a home. Tools, furniture, clothing, and food could all be purchased at the company store. This easy-to-obtain credit proved to be perpetual debt for the miners. Singer Tennessee Ernie Ford summed it up best in his 1955 hit "Sixteen Tons," in which he sang, "I owe my soul to the company store."

As 1941 approached, it became obvious to everyone that the United States would enter the Second World War. Coal was the necessary commodity needed to build the war machine. The time would come during the war when miners were frozen to their jobs. They could not quit their jobs nor be fired. Even though big business would increase profits by nearly 600 percent during the war, miners could not get even a one-cent raise on the hour.

After more than a half century of mining, the easy-to-reach coal was beginning to dwindle. The large coal companies began to pull out in the mid-1950s. The stores and shops closed, and the companies stripped everything that was feasible to take from the community. They even took the fence, lighting, and bleachers from the Weeksbury ballpark. The miners and their families began pulling out as well. The number of children attending Weeksbury's elementary school dropped from nearly five hundred in 1960 to less than a hundred at the end of the decade.

Keep in mind the '50s and '60s were prosperous years for most other Americans. Colossal projects were underway in the United States during those years: the Eisenhower Interstate

Highway System, the space race, and, of course, the arms race. By the end of the '60s, the United States was spending $30 billion per year on the war in Southeast Asia. All this drove industries in the private sector to new and higher levels of production. Cars were being built by the millions, people were buying houses, more people were going to college, and more people were able to achieve the American dream. Not so for those who stayed behind in Appalachia when the large companies pulled out.

A few miners went into business for themselves in an attempt to extract the remaining coal. These small operations were known as truck mines, where coal was produced in small quantities and hauled to the marketplace on trucks versus trains. Large trucks loaded heavy with coal kept the roads muddy and rutted.

The coal industry took its toll on the people as well as the land. Miners were maimed or killed, and many suffered long-term effects such as black lung and other debilitating sicknesses. Very few people in Appalachia were unaffected by the dangers of coal mining. In fact, our grandfather, our mother's father, was killed in a Weeksbury coal mine in 1924. Her mother died shortly thereafter, and then she and her only sibling, our uncle Jim, were orphaned.

Eastern Kentucky is built of small communities, and the people are hardworking and honest. We've had our share of thugs, bootleggers, and crooked politicians, but I'm happy to say we've also had enough good people to keep the bad ones in check. Over the years, people would go about their way, minding their business, until someone became sick or passed away. That's when neighbors would gather to help in any way.

We had good teachers in Eastern Kentucky, knowledgeable teachers who could have taken their education elsewhere and probably enjoyed greater prosperity. For whatever the reason, however, our teachers remained to teach us and prepare us for life outside Appalachia. Those teachers knew the time would come when most of us would go in search of opportunity elsewhere. Most of our teachers had themselves moved to eastern Kentucky from elsewhere or had gone elsewhere to get their education. Hence, they had knowledge of life beyond Appalachia, and they knew curiosity and the search for a better life would take most of us away.

Radio was our primary source for information when I was a kid. We listened to shows such as *Gunsmoke* and *Dark Shadows*. The entire family would go to the fields each day. Our mother and Lily would return home earlier than everyone else in order to prepare the evening meal.

On summer evenings as we walked from the field at 6:00 p.m., we would hear a song called "Suppertime." Jimmie Davis, a former governor of Louisiana, wrote and recorded the song in the early 1950s. The local radio station in Whitesburg had chosen the tune for its theme song. When we heard that song, it was a reminder that the workday was over. I guess we thought that's how life would always be and that we would always be together.

It was lots of fun to gather around the large wooden Philco radio. I can remember hearing John Kennedy's campaign speeches on that radio. We got our first TV in about 1959 or 1960. This was when we first began to see images of the world outside. We saw for the first time images of the desert, the ocean, and, more importantly, the big cities such as New York and Los Angeles. The next thing that happened was a movie theater opening in Wheelwright, just five miles away. Drive-in movies were the next marvel to appear. There was the Almar near Martin, the

Black Cat at Prestonsburg, and the Pollyanna at Pikeville. All this new media provided a view of the outside world as well as a look into the future.

Although we got a glimpse of what life was becoming on the outside, things in eastern Kentucky continued to trail behind the rest of the world. For example, styles for teenagers that were popular in the late 1950s didn't reach eastern Kentucky until the early '60s. A popular song could take a year or more to reach our airwaves.

Our part of the country was somewhat sheltered from the fast-changing world of the 1960s. Race riots and the growing problem with drugs in America appeared to be worlds away. We only experienced these issues on the *Huntley-Brinkley Report,* or we imagined them on TV shows such as *Dragnet.* No one thought much about the war in Vietnam, until local boys began to disappear.

• • • •

A great number of people left Kentucky, never to return, while others eventually came back. Many folks who left the coal fields in the '50s and early '60s began to drift back in the mid-'70s. Most of them had fulfilled their working years and returned home to retire.

But there were noticeable changes in the people who left and then returned. Most of them had a completely different outlook on life when they moved back to Appalachia. Usually, most of the extremely thick Kentucky accent was gone, even if they had only been gone for a short time. This led us to believe there was some-thing in Kentucky they wanted to leave behind or remove from their beings. Some of them acted almost embarrassed by the fact that they had returned. Perhaps they felt they had failed to make it elsewhere and that it wasn't okay to be homesick.

Nonetheless, many returned to look around their hometown and say to themselves that life in Weeksbury wasn't so bad after all. Even if they had to lower their standard of living a little, they would much rather be home.

To live in peace and harmony is all a person should ever have to wish for.

—DALAI LAMA, 1949

Chapter Two

Our family, the Johnsons, lived on 288 acres of land known as Shop Hollow, so named for the machine shop that stood at its entrance. This land, along with a few thousand more acres, had once belonged to our great-grandfather, who sold it to a coal company for fifty cents per acre. There was a condition in the sale that as long as the Johnson bloodline existed, the family would be allowed to live there.

Shop Hollow is a beautiful place with towering mountains on all four sides. There was enough flat land for gardening, and the pasture was fenced about 150 yards up the mountain and was kept mowed and trampled by livestock. Dense forest stood beyond the pasture. Farther up, the mountain fields had been cleared for growing corn, pumpkins, and green beans. It was a great place to be a kid. There was lots of room to run, to play, to grow, and to pretend.

Holbert Mullet had a small grocery store about a mile down the road, but it was a long and muddy mile. I can remember stumbling along that road, trying hard not to fall as I jumped over puddle after puddle. The trick was to stay on top of and between the ruts.

In 1960, the Caleb Fork portion of the road was paved all the way to the entrance of Shop Hollow. This made the trip to the store much easier. Then in 1962, things got even easier when we got our first car. It was a 1955 two-tone blue-and-white Oldsmobile. Neither of my parents ever acquired a driver's license, but that was not uncommon in that area, as they drove only to the store or post office. There were few cars in Weeksbury in those days, and they didn't seem to get into each other's way. Anyway, a driver's license in those days was nothing more than a paper card with the driver's name and address, and as the town constable was illiterate, one could present him almost any kind of card as a license.

• • • •

Four houses were located on the ridgeline the old folks called the Flat Woods (not to be confused with the city of Flatwoods near Ashland). These houses were built high on the mountaintop on the border between Floyd and Pike Counties. It was here our father was born on November 29, 1915. Those houses were accessible on foot or horseback via a trail leading up from Shop Hollow.

He was born with a pioneer spirit that stayed with him throughout his life. Even though he was poorly educated academically, he was very bright in other ways. He was a master of the outdoors. He loved nature and taught us many wonderful things. He knew a great deal about the trees, plants, and animals indigenous to the Kentucky wilderness. He loved to visit the place where he was born. He would tell stories of watching the full moon rise above the mountains to the east. He told of untouched forests, clear water streams, and living in peaceful seclusion. He spoke of a time when he had not yet seen an automobile or an airplane.

The houses in the tiny would-be village where our father was born were gone by the time I came along. Except for a few telltale signs, the forest had all but reclaimed the area. There were some foundation stones, chimney ruins, and bits and pieces of a picket fence. There were, however, a number of fruit trees—a few plum trees, a couple of peach trees, one large apple tree, and one large pear tree. We used to gather fruit from those trees every fall. I swear, it was the sweetest and juiciest fruit you would ever taste. The forest had generated a thick layer of soft black topsoil. Perhaps that was the reason the fruit tasted so fine—or perhaps it was because we were hungry from the more than two thousand feet of steep grade we had just climbed to get there.

We used to gather black walnuts and wild hickory nuts in the fall. On clear autumn evenings after school, we would set out along the cow paths, crunching dry leaves under our feet. Most of the leaves had already fallen, and the goldenrods were beginning to wilt from the first killing frost. "Wait until after the first killing frost, and you won't have to climb the tree," our dad would say. "You'll have to time it just right, or the squirrels will beat you to them." We would make sure the nuts were dried properly and ready for the holiday season. On cold winter evenings, we would crack them on the fireplace hearth.

With the danger of snakes being gone for the year after the hard frost, we knew it was safe to play in the garden among the fodder shocks, which are corn bundles. There were no outside lights, and this made the harvest moon appear much brighter— or perhaps it's only brighter in my memories.

The shadow of the mountain would fall in mid-afternoon in the winter, and my brothers and I would follow the sun's light as it moved up the mountain. We would race ahead of the shadow and play until it caught up with us, and then we would move a little higher up the mountainside. Finally reaching the top, we would watch the sun drop behind the distant mountains to the west. We would then race back down the mountain, stopping long enough to take in the peaceful scene of home. There was blue smoke rising from the fireplace and a warm glow shining from the windows.

There was a creek that flowed just in front of the house. We could lie in bed and listen to the sound of the cascading water. That and the sound of the rain on the roof on a hot summer night were sounds that could put a restless child into slumber better than any sleep aid. It was a peaceful feeling at night when the doors were locked and everyone was safe and in bed. In fact, that was the most peaceful time I would ever know.

• • • •

Our mother was a sweet person. She loved her children, she loved to read her Bible, and she loved flowers more than anyone I know. Her favorite flowers were a group of perennials that grew just outside the living room window along the south end of the house. They would begin to bloom in July and continue to grow to about five feet in height. The flowers were large and bright yellow, probably yellow globes. The flowers would sway in the afternoon breeze and create slow-moving shadows on the floor. This was a soothing effect for a tired kid who was ready for an afternoon nap on the sofa.

I remember giving my mother a deep purple morning glory, and she placed it delicately into her Bible and closed it. She showed me the flower years later. It was thin and dry, but the color had never faded.

• • • •

As a family, we were bitterly poor, but we had so many simple pleasures. We never took those pleasures for granted, but as they say, you don't know what you've got till it's gone. Life was sometimes harsh as well; however, you don't miss what you've never had.

Large families are always fun, and there were several in the area. There were the Mullins, the Mullets, the Sammons, the Bates, and the Skiles. There's no such thing as a lonely child in a large family. We always had things to do. If you ask any members of these families today, they'll tell you they wouldn't have had it any other way.

Simple amenities such as heat, electricity, modern cooking facilities, and fresh water were uncommon in many areas of the coal fields in those days. In many ways, we were all in the same boat, as they say. There were only two classes of people in the coal fields: the poor and the extremely poor. We were among the latter. Of course, there were also robber barons, who owned everything, including the land, houses, stores, and shops. We never saw those people; we only heard rumors of their opulent living.

It was a wonderful community back then. There were no harsh words passed between neighbors, and if a family fell into hard times, then the people of the community would pull together and help out. After all, everyone was in the same situation. We slept in different houses, but we were all the same; we were all one people.

• • • •

It was an innocent way to grow up. We were oblivious to so many things as little children. The area was predominately white, but we had had a few black citizens. There was Old Man Geets, who was just another hard-working and poorly educated coal miner, like the rest of the community.

There was Mrs. Detwiler and her two children. She was about the same age as our mother. I can remember when we would run into her at the general store, she and mother would embrace, and then they'd take a seat on the bench in front of the store. They talked about their gardens and complained about the weather. I swear to you, those ladies never had one good thing to say about the weather. It was always too hot, too cold, too dry, or too wet.

I went to school with Mrs. Detwiler's children. I remember one day when I was about eight years old, the school bus was late for taking us home. I heard whispers from some of the older children that we were going to have to ride the "colored bus." This must be a big deal, I thought to myself, I'm tired of that old bus. When the bus arrived, I was totally disappointed. I turned to my classmates and said, "Well, I'll be a monkey's uncle. It's the same color as the other one!"

In 1964, the Civil Rights Act was signed into law and schools were desegregated. We now had four black children attending our school. Because we were only children, most of us were unaware these children had been forced to go to school elsewhere until then.

Liz Detwiler and my sister Ruth were classmates, and they were the closest of friends. Henry Detwiler was a humble, good-natured kid everyone liked. The other two were Carl and Eric Evens. Nothing humble about those two. Carl was a strikingly handsome boy, athletic and outgoing. Eric, on the other hand, was somewhat of a bully.

I made it perfectly clear to everyone that I wasn't going to take anything from this newcomer. It wasn't long till we had our first fight. There we were, all scratched up and panting like a couple of thirsty puppies, just to get our point across to each other. We must have succeeded, because we became good friends. Eric was much stronger, but the fact was, he didn't want to hurt me any more than I wanted to hurt him.

Boy, how I would love to see those guys today. I often think of the people I grew up with, and I have wondered if I've crossed their minds. Probably not, for I was somewhat insignificant.

• • • •

Life was always interesting—for better or worse—in the Johnson family. A peculiar thing happened on a foggy evening in the autumn of 1962. Our parents were gone, and Lily was at work. Ernie and Linda were in charge; they were fifteen and sixteen years old, respectively. It was dusk—not quite dark, but almost. We were all in the living room playing some silly game when our younger brother, Jimmy, came running in from the other room. He announced that a large black dog was coming up the road toward the house. Jimmy was only about five years old, so we ignored him.

A few minutes later, we heard a sound coming from the kitchen. Ernie went to investigate, with Linda just behind. Linda began to scream, then Marie, then Shirley. I could hear Ernie struggling and yelling for Linda to hand him the poker. We soon found out the "large black dog" Jimmy had seen was a hungry bear, trying to come through the kitchen door.

When Ernie ran into the kitchen, the startled animal began to make his retreat backward through the door. In his haste to close the door, Ernie caught the bear's head in it. It was a tug of war for a few long moments as the bear would push to relieve the pain, and then pull to try and break free. In the meantime, there were two hunting dogs outside nipping at the bear's behind. Today I'm glad for two things concerning that incident: one is that Ernie was as strong as he was, and the other is that Linda didn't give him that poker.

I spoke with Ernie about that incident recently, and I asked him what he thought would have happened if he would have hit the bear with a poker. He thought for a moment, and with a long sigh, he said, "Well, back then, I think that between the dogs and me, we would have whipped him."

Another day I'll never forget is Labor Day, September 7, 1963. Our sister Marie was somewhat theatrical, and she was decorating the barn loft for a play she would perform. She told us to go play somewhere while she prepared the stage. We scattered to the winds to wait for Marie to call us. Not far from the barn was a large sugar maple tree. It was a beautiful old landmark with branches that hung first toward the ground and then upward surrounding the center trunk, almost like upside-down candy canes.

Charles decided he would like to leave his mark on one of the branches, so he climbed about twenty feet to the first branch, where he sat in the bow. He then took a small pocket knife from his pocket and began to carve his initials into the bark at about chest level, leaning in close to the tree and carving upward. Suddenly, the knife slipped, and the point of the blade pierced the pupil of his right eye. Charles dropped his head in disbelief as the knife fell to the ground. Then, the most excruciating pain he had ever felt in his life. Looking back, I'm not even sure how he was able to climb down from the tree, but he did.

Charles was rushed to a hospital in Martin, where he received minimal treatment and was told he would need to be seen by a specialist. The closest specialist was in the town of Hazard, about one hour away.

The news was not good. The doctor said that if the pupil had not been damaged, there might have been hope. The doctor also said the long-term results were unpredictable and that there was a possibility the sight could return perhaps even twenty years in the future.

Charles suffered gravely with severe headaches and dizziness. The trips to Hazard became too many to count. Charles underwent numerous tests, treatments, and medications, but the sight in his right eye never returned.

Charles never let the loss of an eye keep him down, however. He soon began to feel better physically, and the sight in his left eye became stronger, just as doctors had predicted. The accident spoiled his plans to one day be a soldier, as we both had imagined when we were kids. He registered for the draft in 1970 but was turned down. This was the military's loss, for I can attest to the fact that his marksmanship improved to a deadly accuracy in the years following the accident.

What would prove to be the longest and most miserable weekend of my life began on Friday, November 22, 1963. The school fire bell rang at about 1:00 in the afternoon. We thought it was a drill. During a fire drill, the children on the upper level of the building were directed to the back of the building, and the children on the lower level were directed to the front. This time, however, everyone was directed to the front of the building.

Some of the older children were in small groups whispering, and Fay Macintosh sat on the ground crying while her twin brother, Clay, tried to console her. Just then, the sixth-grade teacher, Mr. Robert Smith, called everyone around him and announced we were being sent home early because the president had been shot.

Needless to say, once we got home, the two channels we could get on TV showed repeated images of the assassination. Back then, violence on television, such as a shooting, consisted of an actor grabbing his chest and then faking his collapse. This was different, for this was actual murder on film. It is still one of the most graphic films, to see a beloved president shot with a high-powered rifle.

Mom, Dad, and our brothers Deanie and Sammy were scheduled to leave for a trip to Indiana on Saturday to visit the Lanes. The Lanes were dear friends of our family, and their children had been our friends and playmates for years. But then Fred and Ida Lane left Weeksbury in 1962 for Wabash, Indiana.

Lily would be in charge of things at home while the others left for the trip. I watched the taillights go out of sight on Saturday afternoon as the dreary weekend dragged on. It was good having my older brothers and sisters around. Lily cooked, cleaned, and tried to keep things as normal as possible. We were in a state of shock, yet everyone remained glued to the screen to see what would happen next.

Then on Sunday, it happened again. As Dallas police officers led the suspected assassin, Lee Harvey Oswald, away, a man by the name of Jack Ruby made his way through the crowd and shot Oswald nearly point blank. Nothing would be the same after that weekend. The president was buried on the following Tuesday, and a cold winter soon began.

Nearly three months had passed when things took another turn. On February 9, 1964, the Beatles came to America. Whether we loved them or hated them, the Beatles gave everyone something new to talk about. Although controversial, the Beatles were the distraction the nation needed. Beatle boots, Beatle hairstyles, and all sorts of Beatles paraphernalia could be seen everywhere. If you turned on a radio, their music was on it. Other groups began to appear, and the British Invasion had begun.

Lily had no use for the new sound whatsoever. She just kept to her country and bluegrass, as did most folks in the area. To us kids at school, however, the Beatles were everything. All the girls wanted to hear the Beatles, and all the boys wanted to be a Beatle.

I consider the days of old, I remember the years long ago.

—PSALMS 77:5

PART TWO

Losses

Chapter Three

Before the history of our community and our family leads us to Angel, you must understand that Bill and Lily are no strangers to death. The families in our Weeksbury community have seen many tragic deaths over the years. I find it hard to explain how and why the people of Weeksbury have suffered the loss of so many people.

The people of Weeksbury don't seem to have longevity. Freak accidents or strange, unknown illnesses have claimed so many, as you'll see in the following pages. I've only written about a few of them here, but when I sit down to reminisce with family members, I'm shocked to learn just how many more friends and classmates are now gone.

These people were very close to us all and played a part in our everyday life. There were no strangers in Weeksbury. As mentioned earlier, Weeksbury consists of two hollows, with only one way in and one way out. We grew up in the very last house in the hollow known as Caleb Fork. Therefore, we had to pass at least half of Weeksbury's population every time we went someplace. This kept us extremely close with the community. We didn't go in or out of Weeksbury without stopping to chat with friends and neighbors. These are the stories of the deaths—but also the lives—of people around us.

• • • •

Tragedy often follows families in our community. One such family was the Little clan. We became acquainted with Bill and Ruby Little and their children in 1964. Bill and Ruby had five children: Billy, Jimmy, Teresa, Ricky, and Tammy. Jimmy and my sister Ruth started dating in 1965 and went on to be married in September 1969. They remained married until Jimmy's death in 2006.

Bill had tried his hand at coal mining but found little profit in such backbreaking labor, so he turned to bootlegging. By the time we became friends with them, he had already spent a couple years in the penitentiary for making moonshine whiskey. This didn't make him a bad person at all; he was actually quiet natured and kind.

Bill was no longer involved in the distillation process. He was now, shall we say, a retailer. He only sold the stuff. Bill didn't even transport moonshine anymore. Someone would pick it up in another county, such as Harland or Perry County, and haul it in to Bill. That's not to say we didn't have good moonshiners here in Floyd or Pike Counties, but that would arouse suspicion. Bill would then take his delivered goods and mix up his own concoction with the moonshine in order to double his profits. Bill was quite enterprising in that respect.

After a while, Jimmy took over the job of picking up the load and delivering it to Bill. I or my brother Charles would accompany Jimmy on these mountainous trips. The average load was about eight gallons, and unlike in the movies, we didn't leave the still at breakneck speed. We drove very carefully and never ran unless we were chased. If that happened, then it was a contest between the hauler and the police. Believe it or not, in those days, the hauler often won.

Our parents were completely oblivious to these risky adventures, and I can't believe they never found out. But when Jimmy introduced me to my first beer, my parents knew it the very next day. You see, I didn't know about hiding the symptoms such as cottonmouth or having to pee in the middle of the night. Our parents were so anti-bootleg and anti-alcohol, I shudder to think what would have happened to Charles and me if they had known about our involvement with Jimmy.

Children of bootleggers often gave their fathers' secrets away. This happened at least once with the Little clan. At the beginning of the school year, teachers would have the children come up to the front of the class, introduce themselves, and tell what their fathers did for a living. When Ricky Little was asked about his father's occupation, he didn't hesitate. He spoke clearly and proudly when he said, "My daddy sells the best goddamned moonshine whiskey you ever cracked your bill on."

On one occasion, Jimmy asked for volunteers to accompany him on a trip across Buckingham Mountain to pick up some beer. All the surrounding counties were dry, so even beer was illegal to buy or possess. He was joined by our brother Deanie, as well as two other local boys, Charles and George Dutton. Charles drove on the return trip, as Jimmy sat on the passenger side.

About five miles from home, Jimmy spotted the police, and the race was on. Less than a mile after the chase began, Charles missed the curve and drove the 1966 Pontiac Catalina directly into a large willow tree. George and Deanie were unhurt, but Charles Dutton's head hit the windshield, leaving him scarred for life. Jimmy was trapped in the car until my brother Charles arrived and literally ripped the door from the hinges. Jimmy's left foot had been twisted completely backward, and his nose was almost severed. Jimmy would wear the scars for life. His nose was deformed, and he would forever walk with a limp.

• • • •

Having left Kentucky in 1971, my last memories of Tammy Little were of her as a little girl. Tammy was a cute little thing with long, light-brown hair and dark eyes. I never heard anything more of her until Thanksgiving weekend 1985. It was November 29, to be exact.

Tammy had grown up and was married with a baby daughter of her own. She was out Christmas shopping with her sister-in-law Janis Elkins. They were headed north on US 23 about midway between Paintsville and Prestonsburg when a car driven by Linda Wright crossed the center line and struck them head on.

Tammy was killed instantly, and her baby, one-year-old Maria Lynn, was ejected from the car. The baby was alive but had to be placed on life support. When doctors said there was no hope for the child, the support system was disconnected, and the baby was allowed to die. Maria Lynn was placed in Tammy's arms, and they were buried together in the same coffin.

• • • •

Years passed, and in 2005, Billy Little developed breast cancer. It sounds strange for a man, but it happens more often than you'd think. What's even more unusual is that Billy had always lived a wholesome life. He never smoked a cigarette in his life, and the most I'd ever seen him drink was two beers. He spent his entire life as a teacher, and he always looked healthy and athletic. By the time the cancer was detected, it had already advanced into other parts of his body. The only thing the doctors could do was prolong the inevitable. Billy passed away in early 2007.

• • • •

Jimmy Little's death was unquestionably the most bizarre of all the recorded deaths in the history of Weeksbury. Jimmy had always had a problem with obesity. He stood about 5'10" in height, but he weighed more than 340 pounds. Jimmy never smoked, but he was a beer lover. About ten years before his death, he became diabetic, so he quit drinking and tried to watch his diet. Unfortunately, Jimmy was never one to exercise, and the weight problem persisted.

In the fall of 2005, Jimmy went hunting with my brothers. He got a blister along his waistline from the cartridge belt he was wearing. The blister became infected with some kind of rare flesh-eating disease, and it began to spread. He showed me the wound in early March 2006, and at that time, it was about the size of a dollar bill. Jimmy said to me, "Wynn, I'm afraid I've got something that's going to kill me this time." I asked him what the doctors were saying about his condition, and he said, "They can't even figure out what it is."

I called Jimmy frequently throughout the summer and fall of 2006. He had joined the church, and his outlook on life, as well as death, was good. I have to think that deep down, Jimmy wanted to live. It was only the last month of his life when he realized there was no hope for his survival.

By November 2006, the infection had completely encircled his body. My sister described it as science fiction. My brother Charles told me that for the most part, the only thing holding Jimmy together was his backbone. Everyone who saw him— friends, family, and medical staff alike—marveled at the fact he was still alive.

About two days before his death, Jimmy began to talk to the dead. One day my sister Ruth went to see him at the hospital, and Jimmy stopped her as she was walking into the room.

He said to her, "Ruth I want you to catch Mom before she goes. I want to talk to her about something."

Ruth asked, "Where is she Jimmy?" Jimmy's mother, Ruby, had already been dead for a number of years.

Jimmy replied, "She was walking out as you were walking in."

Ruth said, "I didn't see her, Jimmy."

"She was just here, talking to me," he said. Jimmy Little died the next day on December 6, 2006, at the age of fifty-four.

For all our days pass away under thy wrath, our years come to an end like a sigh.

—PSALMS 90:9

Chapter Four

Another family that saw tragedy was the Lanes. Fred and Ida Lane had four children: Freddy, Mary, Ann, and Ray. As mentioned in chapter 2, they left Weeksbury in 1962 for Wabash, Indiana. They moved away so suddenly, and as children, we just didn't understand.

Freddy and our brother Deanie were best friends. As young boys, they made plans to join the military and serve in a war. Deanie was unable to pass the physical exam, but in 1967, Freddy was drafted. He served for thirteen months in South Vietnam and saw heavy fighting along the Ho Chi Minh Trail. Freddy came home to Indiana from the war, got a job, and was becoming quite successful, but he was killed in an industrial accident.

A few years later, Ray Lane visited Kentucky for the first time since leaving in 1962. He wanted Deanie to take him to Collier Rocks, a towering plateau that stands on the mountaintop in Shop Hollow. It's a place where we played and camped as kids. Falling or jumping from Collier Rocks would mean certain death, and that is exactly what Ray told Deanie he was planning to do.

Ray started toward the edge of the cliff when Deanie stopped him, saying, "Come on, Ray. I thought you liked me."

Ray responded, "You know I do, Deanie. Like a brother. But I just don't want to go on."

Deanie said, "Look, Ray, if you do this, they'll think I had something to do with it."

Ray listened that day. But a short time after he returned to Indiana, he climbed a television transmitting tower and jumped to his death.

In another tragedy, Ann Lane was living in Georgetown, Kentucky, just north of Lexington. She was driving home after attending the Kentucky Derby. She lost control of her car and drove into a lake. Her body was discovered a short time later.

For all flesh is like grass and all its glory like the flower of grass. The grass withers and the flower falls, but the word of the Lord abides forever.

—1 PETER 1:24

Chapter Five

Of all the people who I've ever known, there's never been a family that's seen as much misfortune as the Mullets. Paul Senior and Sarah Mullet had thirteen children: Paul Junior, Nikki, Danny, Ronnie, Shirley, Ricky, Roy, Dennis, Gordon, Tony, Scotty, Teresa, and Homer.

Paul was about twelve years old when he was kicked in the head by a pony. He developed tumors and passed away a few months later. I don't believe his parents ever completely recovered from the loss.

In 1963, while playing with the other kids, Roy jumped from the porch and was impaled on a horseshoe stake. He survived the accident, but only after undergoing extensive surgery and a long and painful recovery.

Ronnie was living in Massachusetts when he was involved in a car crash in 1968 that left him crippled for life.

My sister Lily was waiting for her ride to work early one morning in the summer of 1969 when Shirley Mullet went rushing past. When Lily asked where she was going in such a hurry, Shirley exclaimed, "I'm going to ask Brown Sammons if I can use the phone. Little Scotty's dead!" The brother was about two years old, and it's believed he died from Sudden Infant Death Syndrome (SIDS).

In 1972, their house burned to the ground. No one was hurt in the fire; however, Sarah died just a couple months later.

Danny was at the Ohio State Fair in 1974, where he fell from an amusement ride. He survived the fall itself, but was then struck in the head by the machine and died instantly.

Roy returned home after a tour of duty in the Marine Corps in the early 1980s. About two years later, he shot himself in the head with a .38-caliber pistol.

In 1991, Tony became the first person I knew personally to die from AIDS.

I don't remember Homer—he and little Teresa were the youngest. They were just children when I left the area. However, I was told Homer drank himself to death.

Between morning and evening they are destroyed; they perish without regarding it.
—JOB 4:20

Chapter Six

I guess it must have been about 1964 when I met Joe Allen Berger. He was a good-looking kid, brave and daring. He could be as mean as a snake and prone to sneak a cigarette or a chew of tobacco. Overall, though, he was good-natured and easy to get to know.

Allen, as he was known, grew up to be a fine figure of a man, with dark eyes and a bright smile. He was tall and muscular, not an ounce of fat on him. He somewhat resembled the actor Burt Reynolds.

As soon as he was old enough to work, Allen became a coal miner. It was a job he absolutely loved. It's the same with most miners. To them, there's no better way of making a living. He was taking a long drink from his beer, when I asked him why he liked being a coal miner. He burped and said, "Gets in your blood."

Allen married my sister Shirley in the early 1970s, and their son, Kelly, was born in 1975. Their daughter, Misty, was born six years later in 1981. You could never imagine two prettier children. Kelly was a handsome boy, and Misty's hair was so blond, it was almost white.

I didn't see as much of Allen as the rest of the family. This was simply because I wasn't around as much. But then an event occurred in the last week in September 1987 that led me to spend some time in Kentucky. Shirley called me on a Thursday night to tell me our brother Deanie's house had burned to the ground. No one was injured, but the house was a total loss. Although it was tragic, our response was fairly simple: We're a large family, and there was certainly enough skill within us to rebuild it. So I gathered up some tools and headed to Kentucky.

About three days into the project, an old car with an extremely loud muffler came roaring up the long driveway to the new home site. Allen rolled out, drunker than a hoot, with a wide smile on his face. He said, "Wynn, I heard you were here, so I came to see you." I couldn't believe it was the same person. He had lost weight to the point where he almost looked frail.

We hugged, and then he said, "I'll have to hide my car because if the law finds me here, they'll arrest me." He went on to say, "You probably didn't know that Shirley and I are getting a divorce, and I'm not supposed to be around her."

I asked him how he was going to hide his car, and he said, "I'm going to drive it up above that timberline."

The timberline he was referring to was about two hundred yards straight up and through an old abandoned pasture. I said to him, "Allen, you can't take that car up there."

He said, "Well now, you just watch me." After spinning tires and slinging rocks and dust, he managed to do it on about the third try.

Allen visited for some time but eventually wandered off toward my mother's house. She brewed up a large pot of coffee, and the two of them sat on the front porch and talked until dawn.

The divorce was final by the end of 1987, and I didn't hear much from Allen for the next ten years. In the fall of 1997, he developed an uncontrollable cough, and it was soon discovered that he had terminal cancer. Doctors said it was a combination of coal dust and cigarette smoke that claimed his life. Joe Allen Berger passed away on March 6, 1998, at the age of forty-three.

For the righteous will never be moved; he will be remembered forever.

—PSALMS 112:6

Chapter Seven

In 1966, Lily began working as a housekeeper for the Owens family. They were a family of educators. Marcus Owens Senior was the Floyd County school superintendent, and his wife, Inez, had a dual role as an eighth-grade teacher and Weeksbury's elementary school principal. Marcus Junior was a teacher, and Inez had a sister who taught school as well.

Larry was Inez and Marcus's youngest son, and he was the exception to the family. Larry enrolled in college at Morehead, but dropped out and got a job as a coal miner near Pikeville. Needless to say, this was a grave disappointment for the Owenses. Larry was a good boy—just somewhat of a rebel. Larry didn't mind the rigors of the coal mine; he liked the challenge and the opportunity to prove to his parents he could make a living without a college degree.

Larry lived fast, and he liked to drive fast. If ever a young man set out to burn the candle at both ends, it was Larry Owens. They just couldn't seem to slow him down. He worked too hard, slept too little, and drove too fast. He seemed to be acting out the part of James Dean in *Rebel Without a Cause*. He would often talk to Lily about his troubles, but he kept to himself for the most part. He just stayed in his room, listening to his Eddy Arnold records.

Inez and Marcus worried about his driving more than sixty miles of mountain roads each day to get to and from work. Inez expressed to Lily on more than one occasion her concern. Her greatest fear was Abner Mountain. From the beginning of the slope on the Floyd County side, the road crosses into Pike County at the summit, then comes to a T at Indian Creek Junction. This is a distance of about twelve miles of treacherous mountain driving, with drop-offs and hairpin curves. This was the part of the journey that haunted Inez's worst nightmares. She told Lily repeatedly how she worried Larry would have an accident on that mountain.

Early on a summer morning in 1966, Larry had already crossed Abner Mountain, the bad roads a few miles behind him, when his light blue 1965 Plymouth Valiant slammed into a giant beech tree. There were no skid marks; it's believed he fell asleep at the wheel. Larry was killed instantly.

The entire community mourned the loss. School was out for the summer when the accident occurred, which gave Inez a little time to recover, although she was obviously broken and defeated. Inez returned to work when school resumed in the fall of 1966. Her suffering was obvious, in spite of her effort to conceal it from her class. She was often seen crying and being consoled by other teachers. Friends and coworkers advised her to take more time away from work, but Inez was a persistent lady, and work seemed to be therapeutic.

We teach our children to be strong and independent. However, sometimes they become stronger and more independent than we anticipate. Sometimes our children are mirrors of ourselves, and that's what we want. But sometimes we inadvertently lead them to believe that they must follow in our footsteps. I firmly believe this was the case with Larry Owens. He loved his parents; however, he did not want to mimic their lives or their careers.

I'm absolutely sure Larry would have one day been the quality person his family expected him to be. Even though he showed little interest in college, Larry had a plan for success. He had set out to prove his ability to think for himself and to do things his way. But he worked too hard, slept too little, and drove too fast, and as a result, he and the Owens family paid a terrible price.

• • • •

Weeksbury mourned the loss of another young resident in 1967. Just a few days after school adjourned for the summer, James Preston Hall was riding in a car his brother's wife was driving. The 1964 Ford Falcon convertible drifted into the ditch along the right side of the road and struck a boulder. The car then swerved to the left and over an embankment just high enough to cause the car to flip onto its top. James's head was caught by the rim of the door and pinned to the gravel road.

A crowd gathered and worked frantically to free James. An ambulance arrived about a half hour after the accident and took James to a hospital in Pikeville, where he was pronounced dead. Rescue time was not a factor in the death; he died of severe brain damage. He was fifteen years old.

I think our sister Marie bewailed the loss of James more than anyone, as they had been classmates. We believed James was Weeksbury's rising star. He was strong, athletic, and academically ahead of his class. Coleen Hall loved each and every one of her children, but James was the special one. James Preston Hall neither lived nor died without leaving a legacy—he left something for everyone who knew him.

Sometimes a man who has toiled with wisdom and knowledge and skill must leave it to a man who did not toil for it.
                                        —ECCLESIASTES 2:21

Chapter Eight

Weeksbury also saw violent tragedies. On a quiet Sunday evening in 1969, my brother Charles and I were walking down the road leading out of the hollow when shots rang out. A little farther on, we noticed a car abandoned in the road at the entrance of the hollow. We met our older brother Deanie, who advised us to turn around, as he thought there might be trouble ahead.

The car had broken down, and Deanie had tried to help the passengers. However, the gang of drunken thugs didn't understand the car would have to be towed. They then demanded to use a phone, and Deanie told them no one had a phone in Shop Hollow. The only people with a phone was the Sammons family.

The gang then made their way to the home of Brown and Dora Sammons. Brown and Dora were caring for their toddler grandson while their daughter Maryann was out of state working. Little George was in the yard playing when Ernest Hall came to the door. Brown had zero tolerance for alcohol, and when he refused to allow the gang to use the phone, trouble soon erupted.

When Brown told Ernest he would not allow a drunken person to enter his home, the yelling began. The child became frightened and began to wail. Ernest then called the child a "squalling brat" and demanded that Brown silence him. He then picked up the little boy's tricycle and began to beat Brown savagely.

Fearing for her husband's life, Dora stepped onto the porch with a handgun and opened fire. As the gang fled back down the lane, Dora continued to unload. Ernest was the only one hit in the shooting. He made it a couple hundred yards and then collapsed. Ernest Hall would survive the gunshot wound after surgery to remove a small portion of his liver. Dora had been charged with attempted manslaughter, but after testimony from neighbors who witnessed the incident, all charges were dismissed. The trial lasted only two days.

The gang continued to wreak havoc in the community for several months until the spring of 1970, when they had an encounter with Russell Sloan. This is when fate would have its true retribution.

Russell Sloan was married to my cousin Helen. Russell hadn't done much to prove himself in the marriage, but he was finally working as a coal miner. Russell had caught a ride with a coworker, who dropped him off at the Wheelwright Junction Bridge about a mile from home. No one is sure just why, but the gang attacked Russell. They beat him severely, nearly severing his left ear before throwing him from the bridge into the creek.

Somehow Russell managed to crawl home, but the gang wasn't finished with him. After more drinking, swearing, and boasting, the gang went to Russell's home to finish what they had started. Ernest led the gang up onto the porch, where he braced himself and kicked the door in—only to be met at close range with a shotgun blast to the center of his chest. The remainder of the gang fled. And as Ernest's body quivered, Russell reloaded, stepped over the dying man, and continued firing.

He shot two more of the gang in the backs as they ran, but they survived. Russell was not charged in the killing of Ernest Hall, for he was found inside Russell's home. However, he was charged with attempted manslaughter for shooting the other two men. Russell was sentenced to four years in the penitentiary. My cousin Helen soon divorced Russell and moved to Michigan, where she still lives today.

I've often wondered if the gang would have been a little more merciful when they called Brown Sammons's grandson a squalling brat if they had known he was dying. After treatment at local hospitals, Little George was taken to Indianapolis for radiation and chemotherapy. In spite of all efforts to save him, the child passed away with leukemia in early summer 1970. He was five years old.

The entire community mourned the loss of Little George. The Sammons family was loved and well respected, and we all knew Little George would have been a wonderful addition to their reputation.

As for the gang of thugs and troublemakers, I can think of no better fitting quote than the following.

Hell settles all accounts.

—THE HOLY KORAN

Chapter Nine

Even the Skiles family experienced tragic death. Bill's brother Johnny Ray and his wife, Barbara, lost their son in the spring of 1970. Charles Ephraim Skiles died at home. He was only four months old. It was a completely unexpected death. Charles had appeared to be a healthy child; the only apparent sign of trouble were cold-like symptoms, such as a runny nose. They had taken the child to the doctor, and he was treated for a cold. Johnny Ray's father, Johnny Senior, had been to visit earlier that morning, and he had held the baby and played with him. There appeared to be no signs of sickness at all.

So when Barbara looked in on Charles and found him to be unresponsive and limp, she called for an ambulance, and then she called Johnny Ray's sister Eloise. Eloise rushed to the home just as the baby was being removed. She then called their brother Larry and told him to find Johnny Ray—she rightfully feared the child was already gone.

An autopsy was performed, and it was discovered that the child's lung had collapsed. The child had been suffering from walking pneumonia. The doctors also said he would have probably died even if he had been in a hospital.

Johnny Ray was out fishing with four of his brothers, Bill included, when Larry came and told him he was needed at home.

Larry didn't say why to any of them, but he appeared to have been crying. Johnny Ray left immediately. Soon after, the Springfield police came and said they were looking for a Johnny Ray Skiles. Bill told them Johnny had already left and asked what was going on. The police only added, "There seems to have been an accident, and I would advise all of you to go home."

The Reverend Bob Mead officiated Charles's funeral. As he delivered words of hope, it was obvious that life for Johnny Ray and Barbara Skiles would never be the same. Bill and Lily would find themselves in a similar fate years later.

What can parents do when this kind of tragedy occurs? What can they think, and how can they think of anything else? I have posed this question to parents I've known who've lost children, and there is no answer. What I have been told is that parents will continually flash back in time and remember holding their child. They will have vivid pictures in their minds of the child's most crowning achievements. They remember the proud moments in the child's life, such as learning to read, to spell, or to ride a bicycle. Harsh words, rebellion, or disappointments are never again thought of and are forgotten forever.

Sometimes when death comes to collect, it takes more than its share. In the span of one week in August 2006, Bill learned he was losing two brothers. Within that week, both Ronnie and Gerald were placed on hospice care. Both Gerald and Ronnie were afflicted with mesothelioma, an industrial-related illness caused by asbestos in the workplace. Both were given one week to one month to live.

It's hard to imagine losing a close family member, but try to imagine losing two, and not knowing which would pass first.

On September 28, Gerald passed away at the age of seventy. Lily had called Bill at work and said, "Bill, you need to come home. Your brother passed away."

Bill replied sadly, "Which one?"

Lily then said, "It's Gerald, Bill. He's gone."

Ronnie hung on longer. He lived in West Portsmouth, Ohio, with Gladys, his wife of many years. Ronnie was well respected and loved throughout Ohio and Kentucky. An active member of the church, Ronnie didn't have to be called—he seemed to show up wherever he was needed. Ronnie Skiles was a unique individual. He was always upbeat and positive, never condescending or negative.

I think it was about 1971 when Ronnie joined the church. He attended a seminary school in a small town along the Ohio River near Ashland. Ronnie then became a minister. He attended more funerals than anyone I know. In times of sorrow and bereavement, Ronnie was there to lift spirits and let those suffering know they were not alone.

When I first found out Ronnie had become sick I called him. But Ronnie wasn't just sick—he was dying. For a time, we just made small talk as I tried to avoid the question. Then Ronnie said, "Well, I guess you know they've got me on hospice care."

I then asked, "How long, Ronnie?"

He replied, "They said it could be a week or two, maybe longer." He then said, "It's going to have to be longer because I have to go fishing first."

All I could say was, "Ronnie, this is not fair."

He said, "Wynn, I've had a good life, and if God's ready for me, then I'm ready to go." That was in October 2006.

I was in Ohio for a visit during the holidays that year. Ronnie was watching football, and aside from the oxygen tube, he appeared to be completely healthy. He didn't appear soft spoken or frail—he was just Ronnie. We sat on the couch, watching the game and reminiscing about people and days gone by.

I guess that's why the news of his passing was so hard for me to accept. Ronnie Skiles died on March 27, 2007.

In all the squares there shall be wailing; and in all the streets they shall say, alas! alas!

—AMOS 5:16

Chapter Ten

Tragedy came upon our Johnson family on Memorial Day weekend 1984. It must have been about 3:00 a.m. when my phone rang. The frantic voice on the other end said, "Jimmy Neil's been killed."

It was my sister Shirley. She was saying something about a dune buggy or a dirt bike. Jimmy Neil was our cousin, Uncle Ivan Berlin's twenty-one-year-old son. Everyone just called our uncle I. B.

Jimmy was a handsome young fellow with blond hair and blue eyes. He was a good natured and sensible boy—just a little reckless. He used to ride a dirt bike, which made all of us worry and tell him to slow down, and he eventually gave up on it. He still had a four-wheel dune buggy he used on occasion, though. About midnight on a Friday night, he allowed some friends to take his dune buggy for a short drive. When they failed to return, Jimmy went looking for them. He found the buggy broken down along the road. Details are sketchy, but it's believed that he was attempting to repair the buggy when he was hit by one of his friends driving another dune buggy at a high speed. None of these vehicles were equipped with headlights. Jimmy Neil sustained severe head injury and died instantly.

It's hard to know how a parent is going to react to the loss of a child. Whether a child is one hour old or sixty years of age, the devastation can sometimes cause unexpected and erratic behavior. This was the case with Jimmy's father, our uncle I. B.

He just couldn't move beyond some things regarding his son's death. To begin with, he was convinced there had been foul play involved. The other was something Jimmy had said to his older brother Mickey shortly before his death. The two of them were on the porch talking one day, when Jimmy said something really strange. He said, "Look at the way the sunlight seems to flow over that small knoll over there. You know, that would make a beautiful place for a cemetery." Our uncle owned that land, so Jimmy's body was buried there.

Officials didn't perform an autopsy on Jimmy's body following his death, but I. B. felt performing one would prove or disprove foul play. About a year after Jimmy's death, I. B. had the body exhumed and an autopsy performed. The only findings were that he had been drinking and his death had been nothing more than a tragic accident.

• • • •

As this section about life and death comes to a close, the loss of a loved one is too horrible for most of us to even think about. We think about such horrors only after we have just awakened from a bad dream—or when it becomes reality, and we're forced to face it. I don't think there are any words so beautiful in describing bereavement, bitter loss, and sweet sorrow as the following poem entitled "Annabel Lee" by Edgar Allen Poe.

It was many and many a year ago,
In a kingdom by the sea,
That a maiden there lived whom you may know
By the name of ANNABEL LEE;
And this maiden she lived with no other thought
Than to love and be loved by me.

I was a child and she was a child,
In this kingdom by the sea;
But we loved with a love that was more than love—
I and my Annabel Lee;
With a love that the winged seraphs of heaven
Coveted her and me.

And this was the reason that, long ago,
In this kingdom by the sea,
A wind blew out of a cloud, chilling
My beautiful Annabel Lee;
So that her highborn kinsman came
And bore her away from me,
To shut her up in a sepulchre
In this kingdom by the sea.

The angels, not half so happy in heaven,
Went envying her and me—
Yes!- that was the reason (as all men know,
In this kingdom by the sea)
That the wind came out of the cloud by night,
Chilling and killing my Annabel Lee.

But our love it was stronger by far than the love
Of those who were older than we—
Of many far wiser than we—
And neither the angels in heaven above,
Nor the demons down under the sea,
Can ever dissever my soul from the soul
Of the beautiful Annabel Lee.

For the moon never beams without bringing me dreams
Of the beautiful Annabel Lee;
And the stars never rise but I feel the bright eyes
Of the beautiful Annabel Lee;
And so, all the night-tide, I lie down by the side
Of my darling—my darling—my life and my bride,
In the sepulchre there by the sea,
In her tomb by the sounding sea.

—EDGAR ALLEN POE, 1843

PART THREE

Bill and Lily

Chapter Eleven

It was a different world when my sister Lily was born. Lily was born on March 22, 1941. She was the second child and the eldest female born to a family of thirteen. This position made only one thing certain: Lily was beginning a lifetime of toil.

By the time I was born, Lily had already endured thirteen years of hardship. She never complained about anything. Lily would say it was just the way of life back then. However, I can tell you she shouldered a burden far greater than anyone I know.

As you can imagine, there was always work to be done. Beyond the cooking and cleaning, there were always children for Lily to care for. We were sharecroppers for the most part; hence, farm work had to be done. We had no equipment, so most of the work was done by hand. Harvest time meant food had to be preserved for the winter. This meant cooking, canning, and drying food.

Lily didn't have time for much of a social life, and as she once told me, "Most boys thought I was a young mother with children." She dated a few times, but nothing serious. I can remember one guy she liked quite a bit, but he never made it back from Vietnam.

Lily was always a Christian-minded person and what some today would call low maintenance. She dreamed only of having a home of her own, a husband, and children. I find it interesting that Lily wanted children after all the hard work and worry she endured while helping raise her younger siblings, myself included. Everyone worked in our family, but Lily always seemed to work harder and take on more worry than anyone else. Although I believe Lily is totally unique unto herself, I will admit she could have some inherited traits from our grandmother on our father's side. She's always worried more about everyone else than she does about herself. We've scolded her for worrying too much, but it's never changed her—she's just Lily.

• • • •

When Lily was about nine years old and our oldest brother, Perry, was twelve, they became very involved in the church. Dee and Susann Mullins lived in Shop Hollow, and they had an old open-bed truck they used to taxi the local children to and from church. Lily, Perry, and the other children would sit in the back of the truck and sing songs all the way to and from church.

Perry's always been the quiet one who listens intently before commenting. He is a talented and self-taught musician who has devoted his entire life to his church. He fell in love with a member of his church. Her name was Onida Hall. Onida grew up in a good Christian home, and she was one of the finest people you would ever want to meet. They were married on the twentieth day of June 1960. They have four wonderful children and enjoyed a happy life together until her death in 1990.

Lily and Perry took on certain duties with the church. One of those duties was to look after the sick and elderly. They would carry water from the well, keep the fires going, or do whatever they could to help. They were always there when they were needed. One time they were scheduled to help with a sick neighbor by the name of Russell Hall, but they were delayed a couple of days. This delay would prove to be a blessing in disguise.

Everyone was baffled about Russell's change in behavior. This boy had been mild-natured and intelligent, but was now vicious and hateful. There were even rumors of demonic possession. When there was no other choice, Russell had to be bound to his bed. But he was able to break or slip from his bonds. He would even strike his mother.

Finally, one day the mystery was solved: Russell had been bitten by a bat, and he was dying from rabies. The discovery came too late, however. Russell passed away while he was being transported to a hospital in Lexington.

Russell's parents and all those who had attended him were forced to take a series of painful injections to the stomach. Thankfully, Lily and Perry hadn't be exposed.

• • • •

Lily was nineteen years old when I started to school. She was always up early, making sure her younger brothers and sisters were clean, fed, and out the door on time. We would then walk about a half mile down the hollow and wait for the bus. There was no kindergarten in those days. When a child was six years old, he or she would start first grade. As for Lily, her further education was on hold while she cared for our family.

When Lily was about this age, a strange thing began to happen. She began having recurring dreams or visions of her own child. In the first dream, the child was a newborn. She was holding the child and showing it to her friends and family. When she woke, of course the baby was gone. The dream left her stunned and confused. For days, she just couldn't stop thinking about the dream and the beautiful child she held in her arms that she was so proud of. This was the first of many dreams to come, dreams that were far too lucid to forget even the smallest detail.

A few years later in 1964, Lily had the dream again. The child, a little blond-haired girl, was now three. In this dream, she pulled Lily close, whispering words in her ear, but Lily was unable to understand what the child was saying.

Just a few months later, she had the dream again. The child was now three and a half. The child sat in a school-type chair in this dream, and Lily tugged at her hand in an effort to make her walk, but the child wouldn't leave the chair.

She had the dream again shortly after. The child is now six. The child was wearing a beautiful bright yellow dress as if she were all dressed up for Easter. She was showing little playthings to Lily, but Lily couldn't make out what they were.

• • • •

The final member of our family was born on April 10, 1964. It would mark Lily's first experience walking the lines of life and death with a child.

Just after his birth, Randy developed severe pneumonia. For the first three weeks of his life, Randy struggled for every breath. Lily and my mother were at McDowell Hospital both day and night for what seemed an eternity. They came home just long enough to bathe and pack clean clothing, and then they'd go right back to the hospital.

Randy's condition was so severe, most doctors and nurses simply gave up on him. But not Mother, nor Lily, nor a young doctor by the name of Joseph Deskins. Dr. Deskins worked tirelessly to save Randy's life. It was, as they say, touch and go for the first two and a half weeks. Finally, he began to show signs of improvement, and after three weeks, they were allowed to take him home.

• • • •

In the fall of 1964, Lily moved to Lexington, where she got a job as a waitress in a small drive-in called Jerry's. It was only a short time before she realized she was much needed at home, so she returned to Weeksbury. In addition to helping with our family, Lily found work as a maid for several local families. She worked for Taubee and Winnie B. Johnson, Charles and Joyce Johnson, and Roy and Grace Branham.

Lily soon earned the love and respect of these families. They found her to be honest and hardworking. She in turn developed the same feelings for them with nothing but praise for her employers.

In 1966, Lily began working for the Owens family, who lost their son Larry, as described earlier in chapter 7. It was early 1966 when Lily enrolled in evening classes that she would continue to attend for the next four years. I have to think the Owens family had a lot of influence on furthering Lily's education, as Marcus and Inez were both educators.

During these years of taking night classes, working as a housekeeper, and looking after our family, Lily again had the dream. The child was now seven. Once again, the child took Lily's hand and pulled her close, kissing her on the cheek, and once again, the little girl was sitting and refusing to stand or walk.

The dreams were hard for Lily to understand. The little girl in the dream would show her playthings and then smile, as if she was somewhere waiting for Lily. This gave Lily a strange feeling.

Could this be her future child? Or could it be a warning of some impending disaster that would take Lily to join this child in the afterlife if that was where the child was from?

But the child always appeared happy and playful in the dreams. So Lily convinced herself that this beautiful little blond-headed girl of her dreams would one day be her daughter.

Thereupon I awoke and looked, and my sleep was pleasant to me.

—JEREMIAH 31:26

Chapter Twelve

Bill's family, the Skiles, has known our family for decades. Gary, Bill's brother, was a local boy who had just returned home from the service in early 1966. Gary met my sister Linda, and they began dating. Gary was a stoic but intelligent young man, and when he spoke, it always seemed to matter. The entire family loved Gary. He quickly became a welcome addition to the family. Gary spoke of life outside of eastern Kentucky, and that was something most of us had not yet experienced.

Gary came around a lot. He would bring food items such as hot dogs, and we would roast them on a small campfire. One day, Gary brought pizza. There were no pizza parlors in Weeksbury in those days. This was a packaged Chef-Boy-Ar-Dee pepperoni and cheese pizza meal that had to be mixed and baked. I thought it was the most delicious meal ever.

In September 1966, Gary's brother Bill came home from the service. Bill had just spent a tour of duty in Germany. Lily and Bill began dating on Bill's birthday, September 16.

Bill was the youngest of a large family of boys and one girl, Eloise. Bill was just seven years old when his mother, Sadie Sword Skiles, passed away from complications with diabetes in February 1953.

She had failed to tell her doctor she was having an allergic reaction to medication she was taking for the condition.

Eloise was just a young lady, but she was now the Skiles family matriarch. About two years after the death of their mother, Eloise married Donnie McDavid. While they were still dating, Donnie worked in Chicago and came home to see Eloise on weekends. One day, he told her that if she didn't marry him and move to Chicago with him, then he was going to quit his job and move back to Weeksbury. Like many folks, Donnie and Eloise felt there was a better opportunity elsewhere. They moved to Chicago and later to Springfield, Ohio.

With Eloise in Chicago, this left Johnny, their father, and seven older brothers. The Skiles family was as hardworking and respectable as any people you'd ever want to meet. Johnny was a coal miner. He worked for Eastern Kentucky Gas and Fuel. The older boys would cook, and the younger boys took turns cleaning and washing the dishes.

• • • •

Those were the days of the military draft; thus, it was hard for a young man to get a job until he fulfilled his military obligation. As each boy graduated high school in the town of Wheelwright, he would join the army or the air force.

Bill was an all-American boy. He did well in school and was the captain of the football team. Bill was selected to represent Wheelwright High School in the East Kentucky Mountain Conference football tournament. Even though they lost the tournament, Bill is still proud of the feat. One thing is certain—Bill is a football lover to this day. Bill's favorite sport has always been college football, although as college basketball goes, he also loves those Kentucky Wildcats.

He was twenty-two and fresh out of the army when I met him. Bill was, to say the least, plainspoken and straight to the point. He definitely had the temperament of a soldier. This was something we were unaccustomed to. After all, we were just shy and bashful backwoods kids. Oversensitive, you might say. We wondered who this guy thought he was, telling us not to do foolish things, such as jump through the campfire. Bill soon found a place in our family, as we found the man we all love and respect today.

• • • •

Bill and Gary played an important part in the most memorable Christmas of our lives. On Christmas Eve 1966, we were gathering coal from a mine just over a thousand feet up the mountain. They were predicting snow, and we wanted to be prepared. That morning had been mild and dry, but by early afternoon, a heavy, wet snow was falling. Word came that a member of the community, Noah Cole, had passed away, and they wanted our father to help dig the grave. I kept thinking how untimely it was to lose a loved one at that time of year, what a gloomy Christmas it was going to be.

The snow continued to fall. It was a beautiful snow that stuck to the timber and covered the dark ground with a clean, white blanket. That night, Bill and Gary came, and they brought two sleighs and lots of fireworks which we enjoyed. The night was bright from the falling snow.

Christmas day was bright and sunny. We enjoyed a wonderful meal and were thankful for Gary and Bill, who helped make it a beautiful holiday after all. My brother Charles and I recently talked about that Christmas weekend. I can only hope everyone has a Christmas like ours somewhere in their memory.

• • • •

In the spring of 1967, Bill and Gary left Weeksbury for
Huntington, West Virginia. They were hired by a company called
American Car and Foundry, a company that built railroad cars
for Burlington Northern Railroad. The company had brought in
an additional workforce to fill a rush order, but when the order
was filled, the additional workers were laid off. Gary and Bill were
out of work. After expending their remaining unemployment
benefits, they traveled to Springfield, Ohio. They had relatives in
Springfield, and even though the town was showing signs of the
times, they believed there was a chance for opportunity.

In Springfield, Gary was hired by the Ohio Bell phone company, and Bill went to work for Heat Treating, Inc., a company
that produced steel products. However, Bill's job lasted for only
a couple months, and he was laid off again. Bill then applied for a
job with Robbins & Myers, Inc., which builds industrial-strength

pumps. Bill's starting pay of $2.10 per hour was a little less than he might have made elsewhere, but the benefits were pretty good, it seemed to be stable, and there was lots of overtime.

Bill had plans to use his G.I. benefits to learn a trade in electronics. Robbins & Myers was to be a temporary income until there was an opening in the class at Mayo State Vocational in Paintsville, Kentucky. However, when Bill was called to report for class, he was told that the only opening was for mechanical training, not electrical. He declined the class and remained at Robbins & Myers. When he was first hired in July 1967, I'm sure Bill was unaware he would still be working there nearly a half century later.

• • • •

Springfield is a special place. It's a small industrial town of about one hundred thousand people, situated between Columbus and Dayton along Interstate 70. Springfield was founded more than two centuries ago, and when the first national road was built (US Highway 40), it stretched from Cumberland, Maryland, and ended in Springfield. Hence, Springfield became known as "The Town at the End of the Pike."

By the time Bill and Gary moved to Ohio, Springfield had already seen its economy rise—and fall. Thousands had just lost their jobs when Crowell-Collier (a large printing company) moved out in the mid-1960s. Local downtown businesses were dealt another fatal blow when developers built the Upper Valley Mall just west of town. Then city officials lost a bid for a Campbell Soup canning facility when they failed to come up with a plan to improve the city's water system. Springfield has artesian water that's among the purest to be found, but the problem was the city's inability to deliver it. Actually, Springfield was named by the wife of frontiersman Simon Kenton for the numerous fresh-water springs in the surrounding countryside.

Springfield boasts the home of International Harvester, which opened its doors around 1860 as makers of farm equipment and then trucks. The manufacturing plant was built directly over Mad River, which flows through the center of town. The solid bedrock beneath the river was necessary to support the plant's large steel press used to pound and shape metal. The sound of the press could be heard around the clock and up to a mile away. The city would awaken each morning at 7:00 a.m. to the sound of International Harvester's signature steamship whistle. The whistle would sound again at 3:30 p.m. to end the shift.

Harvester built a new plant in the 1970s, along US Highway 68 just north of town, and by the end of the 1990s, they had deserted the old building. In the early 2000s, the original building was razed, and after almost 140 years, the press and the old steamship whistle fell silent. I visited the former site of the old building in 2005, and with a little imagination, I could see ghostly apparitions of men clamoring through the front gate with lunch buckets in hand. Some men walked slowly, conversing with coworkers and lighting cigarettes, while others rushed to their cars. I then thought of the number of dreams that had been bought or built and the college tuitions that had been made possible there.

Another Springfield landmark stood just in front of Harvester's main entrance. Vining Broom was founded in 1860 by the Vining family. In the 1930s, Vining was sold to the Leventhal family, who expanded the business from manufacturing brooms to producing mops and other types of janitorial products. Among other labels, Vining manufactured the famous Fuller Brush. Vining was passed along through generations of the Leventhal family until 1999, when the business closed its doors in Springfield and moved to Mexico.

Springfield, like many other Midwestern cities, has seen good times and bad but has managed to persevere through the ages. The people of Springfield are proud of many features within the city. There are lots of beautiful churches, several city parks, and theaters. Springfield has a good school system and features two colleges, Clark State and Wittenberg University. Wittenberg is a renowned school and listed as a number one college of liberal arts.

Cultured entertainment can be found just a short distance in any direction from Springfield. Just a few miles south on US 68 is the small town of Yellow Springs, where diners can enjoy a meal in an old tavern that had once been a terminal for the stagecoach line that ran between Cleveland and Cincinnati. A few more miles down the road is Oldtown. For centuries, Oldtown was home to the Shawnee. Nearby, Caesar Creek was named for a black slave who deserted his master and became a Shawnee warrior. Today, you can find almost anything you need at the Caesar Creek flea market.

Just west of Springfield along US Highway 40 is the historic George Rogers Clark mansion. Clark was a general in Washington's army and the father of William Clark, of the Louis and Clark expedition. Clark County was named for General Clark. The annual Clark County Fair is on Highway 41 on the eastern fringe of Springfield, with one of the most impressive agricultural exhibitions in the Midwest. Nearby the Clarence J. Brown Reservoir was built in the early 1970s and offers public hunting, fishing, and water sports.

Spring in central Ohio is a happy but busy time for most people. They hurry about here and there buying this, building that, and planting everything with a pretty picture on the package. They put up fences, paint their houses, and do just about anything they think will catch the neighbor's envy. You might say ambition is born in the spring but then laid to rest in the hot summer sun.

Mid-August in central Ohio is when the rich, green colors begin to dim in the summer heat. New colors begin to appear when the goldenrods and black-eyed Susans cover the land along the roads and fields. Nights become cooler in August, and sometimes morning fog must burn off before a bright sunny day can begin. Shadows are longer, and the days are noticeably shorter.

The mood completely changes by the end of September. Neighborhoods are much quieter now that the children have returned to school. There's something unexplainable in the air. It's time to decorate the front of the house with a sample of the harvest. It seems such a short time now until the Halloween décor is added. Evenings that were spent in the backyard barbequing are now dark and spent watching TV or reading books.

A drive through the country will take you past picture-perfect farms with old but well-kept houses, Sears and Roebuck barns, and carefully manicured landscaping. Farmers with massive machines work feverishly to gather the harvest while the rest of the world slows down to enjoy it. Visiting the farm markets in central Ohio is a must during the fall harvest. You'll find lots of fresh vegetables, fruits, jams, and honey. Black walnuts are scattered along lanes and driveways, while many walnuts still hang from the branches after the tree has lost most of its leaves. Corn, grass, and leaves that have dried in the hot summer sun now emit the unmistakable smell of autumn. The birds are silent now, and the only sound from nature is the crickets—you'll hear just a few crickets at first, almost as if nature is whispering secrets.

Just a short drive to the north on 68 is the beautiful small town of Bellefontaine. Bellefontaine has several family restaurants where you can enjoy home-style cooking. Just ten miles east of Bellefontaine is Mount Victory, an Amish community where things are done in a more traditional way. Horse-drawn carts and plows are still in use, and most of the household furniture and equipment are handmade. Corn stands in bundles, with pumpkins and squash scattered through the fields. Regardless of where they live, whether urban or suburban, visitors to this area tend to sigh and say, "This is how life should be."

The evening came softly, the sun from the western horizon; as if a magician had stretched out his wand turning everything to gold, and the land, the sky and the water melted and mingled together.
—HENRY WADSWORTH LONGFELLOW, 1863

Chapter Thirteen

While working in Springfield, Bill would make the trip to Weeksbury to see Lily almost every weekend, a drive of just over 250 miles. This was not interstate driving, however. It was mostly two-lane highway and lots of stoplights in towns along the Ohio River, such as Portsmouth and Ashland. In good driving conditions, Bill could make the trip in just over six hours.

Lily continued her evening classes and her housekeeping services. Bill and Lily planned to be married as soon as they were sure Bill's job was stable. But there was another issue Lily insisted on resolving before the wedding. Lily had two accounts with local merchants, one for groceries at Mullets and the other for a stove she had purchased at Damron Appliance. All this merchandise was selflessly provided for the Johnson family household. She's often spoken of how wonderful these two merchants were in allowing her the time necessary to pay the accounts in full. Lily worked, attended school, and chipped away at the debt as time dragged on.

And then there was one more matter that very much concerned Lily and made her hesitate in her plans to marry Bill: our youngest brother Randy's health. As mentioned, Lily played a large part in raising her younger siblings, and Lily especially felt the need to be near Randy because he was somewhat weakened by the sickness that nearly took his life as an infant. Randy would have to be a little older and much stronger before she would leave him.

That summer, Lily enrolled at Mayo State Vocational to learn to operate a special sewing machine for the shoe industry. When Lily's training was finished, she was hired at US Shoe in Prestonsburg. The job was piece-rate terms, and Lily sewed six hundred pairs of shoes per day.

Lily didn't have a car, so she would walk to the mouth of the hollow to carpool with a coworker. Lily would leave very early in the morning and not return until well after dark. The walk in and out of the hollow was usually dark and spooky, so my brothers and I took turns walking her to meet her ride.

Prestonsburg was about forty-five miles away, but the trip could take up to two hours. There were school buses and slow-moving coal trucks, and if there was an accident, the road could be blocked for hours. To add to this, there was always road construction or landslides that had to be cleared. It was far from an easy life, but Lily was making more money than she had ever made.

• • • •

Back in Weeksbury, there was a horror-movie marathon on New Year's Eve 1969, and we all stayed up to watch movies and say goodbye to the most tumultuous decade in American history. During the '60s, we saw a president murdered, his killer murdered, a beloved civil rights leader murdered, and a respected senator murdered. We witnessed the hippie movement, racial strife, the war in Vietnam—and we watched it all on TV.

In Springfield, Bill and a friend, John Rains, went to Bill's brother Cleck's house to celebrate the upcoming new year. Cleck had received a bottle of whiskey as a Christmas gift, and they gathered to drink it. Later that night, the booze ran out, so they went to a neighborhood bar to buy beer. But it was too late, and the bartender refused to sell it to them. It was then that the three of them decided they would not enter 1970 with alcohol as part of their lives. The three of them never took a drink after that night, and a short time later, Bill quit smoking as well.

• • • •

Randy was now six years old, and Lily felt he was stable enough for her to go on with a life of her own. In the spring of 1970, Lily and Bill set a date. They would be married on July 11, 1970. I had wondered when this day would come—the day when the circle would break and we would all begin to scatter to the winds. Deanie, Marie, and Perry had long since been married, but they lived close by. Our family had always been close knit, and now Lily was about to move far away. I just hadn't come to terms with the fact.

On Saturday, July 11, 1970, Bill and Lily were married in Clintwood, Virginia. Clintwood is a pretty little mountain village where weddings were a tradition. It had certainly become a tradition in our family. Bill and Lily were the fourth couple in our family to marry in Clintwood. Our brother Ernie married Judy Dorton later that year on Thanksgiving weekend of 1970, and they too were married in Clintwood. Other family members would also marry in Clintwood, including myself.

Lily and Bill would make their home at 425 North Burnett Road in Springfield, Ohio. Lily was homesick at first, but she began to adjust. They would visit Weeksbury every couple of weeks, and Lily was always sad and tearful when it was time to leave. But she was working now, and this kept her occupied. She was working for Springfield Cabinet Works, a company that built kitchen cabinets.

As Bill and Lily celebrated their first anniversary, she had the dream again. The little girl appeared to be about eleven or twelve, but this would be the final dream for a very long time to come. Shortly after this dream, Lily found out she was pregnant. This was the news she had waited for all her life.

The news meant their lives would be changing, beginning with a change in their residence. The North Burnett Road home was a large house divided into three apartments. Lily and Bill lived in the upstairs unit. The property was owned by an elderly couple by the name of Mr. and Mrs. Diebert. Lily and Bill had developed a loving relationship with the Dieberts, but the stairway leading to the apartment was steep, and Lily was afraid of falling now that she was pregnant. So they had to break the news to the Dieberts that they would be moving. The old couple hated to see them go, but the friendship wouldn't end there. Lily and Bill continued to visit the Dieberts for many years to come.

In early 1972, Lily and Bill moved to 320 North Jackson Street—and waited for the day when their child would arrive.

I consider that the sufferings of this present time are not worth comparing with the glory that is to be revealed to us.
—ROMANS 8:18

PART FOUR

Angel's Life

Chapter Fourteen

Angela Rose Skiles was born at 10:27 a.m. on Tuesday, May 2, 1972. Angel weighed 6.15 pounds and was 21.5 inches long. It was a bright and sunny day, but for Lily, it was especially bright. In her thirty-one years, this was without a doubt the happiest day of her life. It was a day she had dreamed of for a very long time.

However, a shadow soon began to form over Lily's bright day. There had been complications with the birth. Angel had been severely cord wrapped. The doctor had to manipulate her before the birth could even take place. There were other problems as well—Lily had toxemia.

For three hours following Angel's birth, Lily was unconscious, finally waking up around 1:30 in the afternoon. Lily and Bill were not permitted to hold Angel. She was taken away and placed in an incubator. Lily would not see her baby for four days.

Dr. Heinrich had long since been Bill and Lily's family physician. He came to see Lily the evening of Angel's birth. Before he could speak, Lily said to him, "Dr. Heinrich, what's wrong with my baby?"

After a long sigh, the doctor exclaimed, "Many things, Mrs. Skiles. There are many things wrong." The doctor went on to say that each and every minute was vital to Angel's survival. He said, "We are counting minutes, Mrs. Skiles, we are not counting hours. She's here with us today, but she could be gone tomorrow. Every minute she lives will strengthen her and increase her chances for survival."

On the fourth day following Angel's birth, a nurse came into Lily's room and noticed she was crying. "What's wrong, sweetie?" the nurse asked.

Lily said, "I want to see my baby."

The nurse then said, "What, honey? Do you mean to tell me you've not even seen your baby?" The nurse left the room, returned with a wheelchair, and took Lily to the nursery to see Angel.

It was then that Lily realized the severity of Angel's condition. Angel was a beautiful but frail little thing with lots of dark hair that would later turn blond. But Angel was almost purple in color, and her breathing was labored.

That night, the nurse told Lily they were having trouble getting Angel to eat, and she asked Lily to try. Lily was able to get Angel to take two ounces of milk, and Angel's condition improved almost immediately.

Finally on the fifth day, Lily and Angel were discharged from the hospital. They had both been very sick, and it was about two weeks before Lily completely regained her eyesight.

• • • •

The summer of 1972 was an unusually cool season. On the Fourth of July, the Skiles family was having a picnic in the park and wanted Lily, Bill, and the baby to attend. Lily told Bill she wanted to go but felt it was too cool to take Angel out into the weather. She also had noticed Angel seemed to be having trouble breathing, so they called Dr. Heinrich, who instructed Lily to bring Angel into his office.

It was just a short drive to Dr. Heinrich's office on North Limestone Street. He worked from his home. Dr. Heinrich was a brilliant but aging man of German decent. He was Donnie and Eloise's family doctor, and they had recommended him to Bill and Lily a few years earlier.

After examining Angel, he instructed Bill and Lily to take her to the hospital immediately. Angel was suffering from pneumonia, diarrhea, and an ear infection. Three specialists were called in: Drs. Gyton, Parsons, and Russell.

For almost two weeks, Angel was in critical condition with little hope in sight—until one morning at about 6:00 a.m. This was when the hospital staff changed shifts. It was usually a noisy time of day; however, that morning was unusually quiet. Lily was looking out the window at a large cross on the roof of a nearby nursing home.

Suddenly, an almost sardonic voice said to her, "Why are you crying?"

This startled Lily and angered her. She said, "My baby is laying there dying, and you're asking me why I'm crying?" But when Lily turned, she was astonished—no one was there.

The next day, Dr. Heinrich came in to examine Angel. A pleasant look spread across his face. He left the room and returned with the three specialists. The doctors were amazed at the findings. Dr. Heinrich then said to Lily, "The pneumonia has broken, and you may take your baby home now."

Lily couldn't hold Angel when she became sick at times like these. Instead, she would sit at Angel's bedside and hold her hand. This was something Angel became accustomed to, and throughout her life, she wanted Momma to hold her hand whenever she got sick.

People would ask, why did this happen? Why is it that some people are having children and giving them away or throwing them into Dumpsters, while people such as Bill and Lily want a child more than anything else in the world but their child was born with inabilities?

These are questions most of us have learned to ignore over the years. For those of us within Angel's realm, we didn't see a burden—we saw a family member, but a special one. Who in the world could have predicted one little girl could have changed so many lives?

Without saying a word, Angel Rose was able to transform so many people. Angel Rose would never forget you. She had certain little signs and motions she recognized people with. I can't explain it. Angel had a way of touching a person's soul—even an agnostic such as me.

Who does great things and unsearchable, marvelous things without number.

—Job 5:9

Chapter Fifteen

Lily, Bill, and Angel lived at the North Jackson Street location for less than a year; it was time to buy their first home. There was a new subdivision being built on the north side of Springfield called Northern Estates. They were small but modern, comfortable homes. Lily and Bill's application was accepted, and construction began on their home on Sudbury Street. The price tag was $70,000. The home included three bedrooms, one bath, and an option between a single-car attached garage or a dining room. Being the homemaker she is, Lily wanted a dining room.

Throughout the summer of 1972, they would drive past their new home to check on the progress. Finally on the first day of October 1972, it was time to move into their new home. Lily remembers how large the home appeared to be and that they didn't have enough furniture to furnish it. Little by little, she soon had things just the way she wanted.

Angel was just five months old when they moved into their new home. Years later, Lily and Bill would own a getaway property in Kentucky, but the Sudbury house would be the only home Angel would ever know. Angel always enjoyed short weekend trips to visit relatives in Kentucky; however, she was always happy when they returned home.

Angel's health seemed to improve after the move to the new house. Lily and Bill attribute this to the lack of trees at the new location. Landscapers placed one small maple tree with a trunk about the size of a half-dollar coin directly in front of each house in the new addition. In contrast, the North Jackson home was located in a very old neighborhood deeply shaded with large trees. Much of Angel's health problems were respiratory, so the dryer environment improved her ability to breathe.

But then during one of the many visits to Dr. Heinrich's office, he noticed something unusual when he listened to Angel's heart. He scheduled an appointment for Angel at Children's Hospital in Columbus. He wanted Angel to be examined by a team of specialists, including a neurologist, a urologist, and a cardiologist.

On October 17, 1972, the doctors found that Angel had a leaking valve near her heart that would probably require surgery in the future. They also found problems with her kidneys. It was during this visit that Angel was diagnosed with a rare syndrome known as Rubinstein-Taybi as well as a syndrome called Progeria, or rapid aging, although her Progeria was mild. This, among other ailments, meant Angel's ability to learn would be slow and she would require special care.

Early in November 1972, Lily made an appointment with Dr. Heinrich to tell him Angel's epileptic seizures had worsened. Per the doctor's instructions, Lily had been giving Angel two types of medicine for the condition (phenobarbital and Dilantin).

Once again, Dr. Heinrich was skeptical. He said, "I don't understand, Lily. These two medicines should have taken care of the problem."

During that same office visit, Angel had an attack. The doctor then said, "Okay, Lily. Let's have her admitted. I want a specialist to examine her. His name is Dr. Chatta—he's a neurologist."

Angel was taken to Mercy Medical Center in Springfield. After three days in the hospital, Dr. Chatta came in to examine

Angel. However, it was not much of an examination. The doctor simply looked at Angel, shook his head, left the room, and didn't return. The next day, Angel was discharged from the hospital.

Again, Lily made an appointment with Dr. Heinrich. When Lily expressed her disappointment with Dr. Chatta, Dr. Heinrich attempted to defend the neurologist. He said, "Well, you see, Dr. Chatta is somewhat shy, and he suffers from a speech impediment." This was about all Dr. Heinrich had to say concerning Dr. Chatta. Nevertheless, Dr. Chatta was never again recommended.

During this same visit, Angel had yet another seizure in the doctor's presence. The doctor drew a deep breath, exhaled with a sigh, and said, "This baby can't live this way." He went on to say, "There's another medicine that has been around for about ten years called Tegretol. I've followed the effectiveness of this medicine, and I think that you should consider trying it."

The medicine was a success, and Angel soon began to stabilize.

• • • •

Family members made every effort to help Lily and Bill when Angel was sick. However, the distance from Weeksbury to Springfield made it difficult for the Johnson side of the family to be with them as often as they were needed. This is not to say they didn't try. Our family had heartfelt love and worry for Bill, Lily, and Angel Rose. We gave help and support in any way we could.

Bill's family was closer and could be within reach whenever they were needed. Within the Skiles family, the hero was Eloise. Eloise—or Sis, as her brothers called her—was to the Skiles family what Lily was to the Johnson family. Eloise was born on July 19, 1931. She and Donnie were married in 1955 and had four children: Rick, Carey, Don, and Tonda.

Eloise and Donnie lived on Revels Street in the same

subdivision as Bill and Lily and could be there in minutes whenever they were needed. Regardless of the time of day, Eloise would be there. From the time Angel was born, she gave more than just another concerned family member. Eloise displayed the love and worry usually only the mother of a sick child could feel. Just like Lily, Eloise watched Angel's every move to learn the signs and symptoms that would tell them she needed immediate medical attention. Whenever days in the hospital became weeks, it was Eloise who relieved the burden. She would urge Lily to try to rest or at least go home from the hospital long enough to refresh herself.

Eloise would sing to Angel, and this, too, was something Angel became accustomed to. One time Eloise had laryngitis and couldn't sing when she came to see Angel, and Angel was noticeably affected.

I guess I can't stress just how much help Eloise was in those days of worry and confusion.

• • • •

Bill was working long hours at Robbins & Myers. The company gave him almost unlimited overtime. This helped make ends meet, as Lily hadn't been able to return to work after Angel was born. It was not unusual for Bill to work twelve-hour shifts and seven days a week. Bill once had an opportunity to work for International Harvester at a higher rate of pay; however, he didn't want to jeopardize the healthcare plan he had with Robbins & Myers.

One day while Bill was at work, a young reverend knocked at their door. When Lily answered the door, the man said, "Hello, my name is Reverend Edward Walters, and I was wondering if I could share some scriptures with you." It was not in Lily's nature to let a stranger into her home, but something in this young man's face told her it was okay.

Lily welcomed the reverend in, and he said, "Before we begin, Mrs. Skiles, I would like to ask you if you have accepted Jesus as your Lord and Savior."

Lily responded, "Yes, many years ago."

After they had talked for some time, Reverend Walters ask if he could return when Bill was home and speak with the two of them together. Lily said to him, "I'm not sure—my husband is a little set in his ways. But I will certainly ask him."

Bill Skiles is plainspoken and assertive, to say the least. Whether politics or religion, no one will succeed in spoon-feeding anything to him. When Lily approached Bill about the reverend coming to visit, he said, "Lily, you tell that preacher I'm a hypocrite." In other words, he wanted nothing to do with Reverend Walters.

A few days later, there was an unexpected knock at the door, and it was Bill who answered it. Surprisingly, Bill welcomed Reverend Walters in, and before he left, Bill and Lily had knelt and prayed with him.

Reverend Walters was a wonderful person, but as a minister, he was somewhat lacking in some areas. Reverend Walters appeared to be more of a teacher than a preacher. The other problem was that he didn't have a church. Even so, for the next few months, Lily and Bill attended services at the reverend's home.

One thing the reader must understand is that unlike the Catholic or Lutheran religion, one could spend a lifetime attending a Baptist church and still be a sinner. It is only after the person undergoes the baptism ceremony that he or she is considered saved. Before one is baptized, he or she must be willing to accept what are probably the strictest guidelines in religion. After a person is baptized, he or she must refrain from any act that may feel like a sin.

This was not a difficult transformation for Bill, for he was honest and hardworking, and he didn't drink or smoke. Lily and Bill continued to attend church with Reverend Walters wherever services were held. The small congregation began to share a church with the Northside Baptist Church, and it was there that Lily and Bill were baptized on April 15, 1973.

But something still seemed to be missing for the Skiles family at the Northside Baptist Church. So one day in the summer of 1973, they entered the Forest Valley Free Will Baptist Church and sat down in a rear pew. After the services, four members of the congregation approached them. Those members were the Reverend Bob Mead, Bob Hawkins, Estill Williams, and Sam Spradlin. The four welcomed Lily and Bill and asked if they would consider joining their congregation. During the conversation, they learned that Reverend Mead had officiated the funeral of Bill's nephew who passed away in the spring of 1970. The Skiles were happy for they had found just what they had been looking for.

For whatsoever things were written aforetime were written for our learning, that we through patience and comfort of the scriptures might have hope.
                                    —ROMANS 15:4

Chapter Sixteen

On the second day of May 1973, Bill was at work when Lily and Eloise celebrated Angel's first birthday with a cake. Boy, did she make a mess of that cake, Lily remembers.

It had been a year of sleepless nights, fatigue, worry, and confusion. Even though Lily had extensive knowledge in caring for sick children, this was different. She, Bill, and Eloise had spent a full year learning medical terms and treatments the average parent does not have to learn. It had been several months since Angel's last hospital stay, and Lily and Bill were feeling a little more assured that Angel would grow up to be strong and healthy.

Dr. Heinrich had played the part of the teacher. He was ever so patient with Lily and Bill, but especially with Lily. He would often say, "Now, Bill, you wait in the lobby, and we'll call you when we are finished." The doctor would then proceed to say, "Now, Lily, this is what you must do." He would then give Lily carefully laid-out plans for scheduling and dosages. He would tell her what she might expect to see in the near future. Dr. Heinrich always had a backup plan, just in case the primary plan proved to be an ineffective solution.

There were several doctors who refused to believe Angel would survive her first year of life, but Dr. Heinrich never showed one hint of doubt. He was like a cool-headed airplane pilot having mechanical problems; he didn't think about crashing, only about

making his plane fly. We've all seen the good old-fashioned country doctor portrayed on TV or in the movies. Well, Dr. Heinrich was just such a doctor in real life. And yes, he made house calls.

His wife of many years also worked in the medical field. Mrs. Heinrich was a nurse at Children's Hospital in Columbus. Just like her husband, Mrs. Heinrich was a kind and gentle person. Even when Lily and Bill called in the middle of the night, she was never at a loss for tender words of understanding. They made a great team, those two. It was as if fate had joined the two of them together for the sole purpose of saving Angel's life.

• • • •

Production at Robbins & Myers had decreased a great deal by the beginning of summer 1973. Then one day, Bill came home with the somber news he had been laid off. He probably could have found another job, but with Angel's medical expenses, he simply had to hold on to his current health plan. With Angel's medical history, it was very unlikely they would have been able to obtain coverage from another insurance provider.

Bill and Lily had no choice but to apply for public assistance. They were given food stamps, but no other assistance was available to them. There were times when all they had were one-course meals, but their faith never faltered, not one morsel passed their lips before they gave thanks and praise.

Bill has always been a person of extremely strong character. He'll find something positive in every situation. Even as I write this, I can hear his voice saying, "Well, that's just how it is" or "We'll just have to get by." This says a lot about Bill's family and the way he was brought up. The same positive attributes can be found throughout the Skiles family. They never seem to complain about anything, not even if they become gravely ill.

Bill applied for unemployment benefits, but that too soon expired. Robbins & Myers would call Bill to work for a couple of weeks, and then they would lay him off for two weeks. Bill was patient and would drop everything and report for work whenever he was called. Bill's work at Robbins & Myers was somewhat feast or famine. He would often work long hours of overtime then find himself laid off for weeks and sometimes months. Union contracts would expire about every three years, often resulting in long strikes and picket pay that averaged about one third the amount of his regular pay. But somehow they managed to keep food on the table.

They were forced to watch every penny. Bill always had something stashed away for rainy days, and as Lily once said, "We had a lot of storms in those days." Somehow news of their hardship reached a church member, Bob Hawkins, one of the first members to welcome them that first day. Just when they were sure they were going to lose their house, Bob presented them with a cash donation. To this day, Lily considers this a miracle.

• • • •

As the days became weeks and then months, there were numerous doctor visits. There were long days and nights spent in hospital rooms. For this reason, Bill found it necessary to ask for a change of shift, as Robbins & Myers operated around the clock. He would now work from 3:00 p.m. to 11:00 p.m. This would enable him to attend daytime doctor visits and drive Angel to Children's Hospital in Columbus.

• • • •

A lady by the name of Patty Evens came to visit Lily in the summer of 1973. Patty wanted to introduce her daughter Holly to Lily. There were only two known cases of Rubinstein-Taybi Syndrome in the state of Ohio. Angel was one case, and Holly was the other. Holly was a few years older than Angel, but they soon became friends. Lily has never met Patty's husband, Don, but she and Patty are very close friends to this day. Patty openly wept when Lily called to tell her Angel had passed away. Now Holly, too, is developing chronic kidney problems, and I pray not, but fear that Holly will be the next victim of Rubinstein-Taybi.

• • • •

By the end of 1973, Angel was still unable to sit alone or hold her head up. Lily would prop her up with pillows to help her sit up, and this began to strengthen Angel. Angel required around-the-clock nursing skills, and Lily and Bill had to administer them. Her breathing had to be monitored, and medicine had to be given. When Angel became sick, they would call Dr. Heinrich, and he, too, was on-call twenty-four hours a day and seven days a week.

For in thee is the fountain of life; in thy light do we see light.

—PSALMS 36:9

Chapter Seventeen

It's important to stress Angel was fun to be around. Even when she was a little girl, she would make cute little gestures we can never forget. Each and every person Angel met was treated differently, as if she developed a different personality for each new friendship. Angel was always smiling and humorous. I used to tease her I was going to bust her in the nose, and she would laugh till she cried.

The old adage "you have to crawl before you can walk" didn't apply to Angel. When she was two years old, she couldn't sit alone or hold her head up, but she could crawl at an incredible pace. They had to keep a pretty close eye on her, for she would get into mischief. She resembled one of those little dolls that crawl. Nothing went unexplored. Angel Rose was fascinated by everything. She enjoyed life to its fullest, never bored or unhappy about anything. We've all seen children become restless, bored, and then cranky. This didn't happen with our Angel Rose. Throughout her life, she was always upbeat and happy, even through the last moments of her life.

• • • •

April 4, 1974, was a typical spring day in central Ohio. There had been some showers and thunderstorms throughout the day, but nothing ominous in the clouds. It was late in the afternoon when Lily drove just a few blocks to the grocery store. But during the short time she was in the store, the sky changed. There were unusual colors in the sky, the clouds were beginning to swirl, and there was a strange roar in the atmosphere. Lily jumped into her car and raced home. Bill met her at the door with an unusual look on his face and said, "Xenia has just been destroyed by a tornado, and there's more on the way."

Xenia is a town of about twenty thousand people seventeen miles to the southwest. The twister had narrowly missed Riverfront Stadium on the Cincinnati Reds' opening day, when the ballpark was filled with fifty thousand baseball fans, including President Nixon.

The storm was a mile wide when it slammed into Xenia, with winds estimated at more than two hundred miles per hour. The winds were powerful enough to blow a freight train from the track, and they threw a semi-tractor onto the top of a building. The storm decimated everything in its path.

Another tornado was sighted close to Yellow Springs, only six miles away. Lily and Bill remained in front of the television to watch for new developments. Bill's cousin Crittie Sword lived in Xenia, and Bill was very concerned about him. As you can imagine, though, all communications lines were down.

Night began to fall in Xenia soon after the twister passed. The town was pitch black as rescue workers searched through the rubble. There were screams, moans, and faint cries for help as the long night dragged on. Live wires were not too much of a concern, but ruptured gas pipes spewed fumes into the open air. Dazed and confused residents wondered about searching for loved ones, while family pets searched among the ruins for homes that no longer existed.

As a new day dawned, unspeakable images began to appear on the TV screen. Witnesses told incredible but true stories of the tornado over and over again. It was as if telling their ordeal would make it somewhat easier to accept.

For the next few days following the storm, the weather was unseasonably cold. Weeks would pass before anyone was allowed to enter Xenia unless they lived there. Countless homes and businesses were destroyed, and thirty-four people lost their lives.

Xenia was not the only city to be hit on April 4, 1974; it was to date the worst tornado outbreak in history. The National Weather Service reported 148 tornados April 3 through April 4. As for Xenia, the city would be hit by another tornado in 1989 and again a few years after that. Fortunately, those two twisters were not as devastating as the storm of 1974.

Lily and Bill were fortunate not to have been hit. There were no basements or any type of safe-rooms in the subdivision where they lived. If a tornado had struck there, the results would have been disastrous.

Out of the south cometh a whirlwind; and cold out of the north.

—JOB 37:9

Chapter Eighteen

In the fall of 1974, Angel developed a severe kidney infection, so Dr. Heinrich scheduled an appointment with a urologist at Children's Hospital. Lily and Bill can't remember the doctor's name, but they will never forget his demeanor. Just moments before the doctor examined Angel, she had been crawling all over the floor of the hospital room, getting into mischief. Then the doctor came in and said, "Why worry about her kidneys? She won't live for long, anyway. Just look at her—she's nothing but a vegetable."

I can't imagine any parent who wouldn't be outraged at such behavior from a physician, and Lily was no exception. By the time they were in the parking lot and Bill prepared to drive away, Lily said, "Stop, Bill! I'm going back in that hospital. No one's going to talk the way that doctor talked about Angel!"

Bill asked, "What are you going to do, Lily?"

Lily replied, "You just watch me."

"Now, Lily," Bill said, "if you go back in there as angry as you are, you're going to get thrown in jail." As usual, Bill was the voice of reason.

There were only a few incidents such as this, for there were also wonderful doctors and nurses. Dr. Wright, a neurologist, was a kind and gentle person. Both Dr. Contras and Dr. Sommers would get down on the floor and play with Angel.

Angel's illnesses never subsided, but by the end of 1974, she was crawling more and more. This was a newfound freedom for her, and she began to explore. She was so cute. She crawled from room to room, inspecting and playing with everything she found. This gave us all a new sense of hope, but the hospitalizations and doctor appointments continued. Lily saved each and every hospital wristband, and she recently counted thirty-nine of them.

• • • •

Bill was hired back on at Robbins & Myers, but the job continued to be unstable. There were contract disputes between company management and union officials, which meant strikes and layoffs. What made the situation seem even worse to Bill and Lily was that it was Christmastime. The church came to their rescue with a contribution of more than $300. That was a considerable amount of money in those days. They were able to pay some bills and have a Christmas for Angel, thanks to those wonderful people of the church. But to Lily and Bill, this was more than a gift from thoughtful and generous people—it was a godsend. Once again, Lily was convinced it was a miracle.

God also bearing them witness, both with signs and wonders, and with diverse miracles, and gifts of the Holy Ghost, according to his own will.
                                                    —HEBREWS 2:4

Chapter Nineteen

Angel loved long evening strolls, and she really loved the sound of the birds. It was a neighborhood of mostly young parents with children, and Angel enjoyed watching the children play. Lily would place her in her stroller, and away they would go.

Angel enjoyed being outside even when the weather was miserably hot or cold. Due to her throat condition, they never kept her out in the cold longer than they had to. Angel's health was always delicate to sudden temperature or climate changes.

Summer heat was, therefore, an issue for Angel. The house had not been equipped with an air conditioner, and the lack of trees made the heat almost unbearable. Lily would take Angel on a stroll in the early evenings to try to escape the heat. Lily longed for the day when the little tree in front of the house would grow large enough to provide shade.

There was a swing set that sat across the end of the driveway, and spending time in her swing was one of Angel's favorite pastime activities. While visiting our family in Kentucky in the mid-1970s, Lily dug up two small vines from a pink rambling rose. She planted one at each end of the swing set, and within two years, the vines had created a box-like tunnel over the swing set. On the third year, a second swing set was added, and the rose vines became a thing of beauty as well as shade.

Somewhere, somehow, someway, Lily was determined to have a vegetable garden. It just so happened the neighbor in back was selling a small garden tiller. His asking price was $50. Bill and his brothers pitched in together and bought the tiller, which they would all share. Lily chose a thirty-by-thirty-foot square directly behind the house, in the northwest corner of the lot.

You'd be amazed at the amount of vegetables they grew in that tiny garden. They had fresh tomatoes, potatoes, green beans, carrots, and other vegetables throughout the summer and fall. They gave baskets of vegetables to friends and family, and they even had enough for canning when the growing season was over.

They had their garden for a number of years. Then one day, a new family moved in next door and planted a maple tree in the back corner of their yard, next to the garden. It was a fast-growing tree, and within just a few years, the branches began to shadow the garden. It wasn't the shade that created the problem; the sap that dripped from the tree simply poisoned the garden.

The family who planted the tree soon moved away, and then Bob and Doris Peets moved in. Lily and Bill soon became very close friends with the Peetses. The Peetses were the very best of neighbors who would do anything for anyone. Out of love and respect for Bob and Doris, Lily and Bill never mentioned the problem with the tree. Lily and Bill eventually gave up on their garden and replanted the site with grass.

Lily enjoyed talking to Doris, and there were many summer evenings when the two of them would stand in the yard talking until the mosquitoes became too much to bear. Bob was a wonderful neighbor. He knew Bill was working long hours, so he would mow the grass in the summer and remove the snow from the driveway in the winter.

Doris passed away several years before Bob; however, he remained active in the church as well as in other hobbies. He had a battery-powered wheelchair, and he would ride it to a local nursing home about a mile away, where he would conduct classes on Biblical scriptures. Bob Peets would remain a close friend and wonderful neighbor until his death in the spring of 2011.

Lily and Bill's gardening endeavors didn't end altogether. They planted fruit trees and hardy, fast-growing flowers. Everything they planted seemed to flourish. Everywhere you looked, there was some kind of tree or plant growing or hanging from pots.

Lily planted some kind of large-leaf vine in a window box inside the dining room. The vine climbed the curtain to the ceiling, then along the ceiling through the kitchen and into the living room, where it turned downward to the floor. Stretched out, the vine would have easily been between forty and fifty feet long. It resembled a sweet potato plant, but no sweet potato plant ever grew that long. Visitors marveled, and everyone asked if the vine was real, but no one ever guessed what kind of plant it was.

The yard was planted with perennial flowers that would bloom from late spring until frost in the fall. There were roses, Rose of Sharon bushes, hollyhocks, yellow globe, and lots of others. The yellow globe was our mother's favorite, as mentioned in chapter 2. In fact, Lily had transplanted these flowers from Kentucky. The yellow globe had long been a tradition in the Johnson family. Through the generations, our family has passed them along. I have some growing in my yard in Minnesota.

In addition to flowers, Lily and Bill had beautiful fruit trees in their yard, which they had planted soon after they moved into their new house. They have a flowering crabapple tree, a peach tree, and several cherry trees. Soon the trees began to flourish. The cherries were especially bountiful. After picking all the cherries they could use, there was still plenty left for the birds. It is a gorgeous sight when those trees bloom in the spring. People passing by will often stop to look, ask questions, or even take pictures.

Whoever is able to make two ears of corn or two blades of grass grow on a spot of ground where only one grew before deserves more of mankind and does a greater service for his country than a whole race of politicians.

—JONATHAN SWIFT, 1726

Chapter Twenty

Everything Bill and Lily planned was done so tentatively. Each and every day of Angel's life was planned according to her well-being. I couldn't count the number of times I heard them say, "We're going home for the holidays—if Angel is feeling all right." On several occasions, they would make the trip to Kentucky to visit relatives, then Angel would become sick. They'd have to cut their trip short to rush Angel back for medical treatment.

Life with Angel meant planning for everything, including the unexpected. The last week in January 1978 had been unseasonably warm and mild in central Ohio, with temperatures in the upper 60s. Anyone familiar with weather in the Midwest would know something was amiss. Forecasters were predicting a swift change in the weather, so Bill thought he better stock up on a few things, just in case of the unexpected.

It all started with rain through the day on Friday, then the temperature began to drop. By midnight, it was in the teens. Weather officials noted the lowest barometric pressure ever recorded to date for the area. A powerful northwest wind was blowing steady, and gusts were reported at more than eighty-four miles per hour.

The house was shaking, and the sound outside was a constant roar. Bill got up at about 2:00 a.m. to see how much snow had fallen, but he was unable to see anything. There was absolutely no visibility whatsoever—not even the streetlight just across the street. The next day, the storm had died down a little, but snow squalls with blowing and drifting continued for the next two days. Some people were trapped on highways, while others were trapped in their homes. The National Guard was called out to remove snow and search for people in need of help. There were cars and even some houses completely buried.

With the blowing and drifting, it's hard to say how much snow actually fell, but drifts were still more than ten feet deep in March. The January 1978 blizzard is said to have been the worst winter storm in a century. It's still talked about today.

With transportation at a standstill for days, Lily and Bill felt they were truly blessed Angel didn't have any major health episodes during that time. Bill was laid off from his job then, so the only thing they could do was, for lack of a better word, hibernate. They had recently purchased a chest freezer and stocked it with lots of meat and frozen foods, so they were better off than some people. Others were caught completely by surprise by the storm.

It's Bill's nature to be as prepared for the unexpected as anyone I know. He's not a so-called doomsday theorist or worrywart; he's just someone who greatly enjoys life yet tries to imagine a worst-case scenario. This has enabled them to outlast a great number of incidents that could have been much, much worse.

Have you entered the storehouses of the snow, or have you seen the storehouses of the hail, which I have reserved for the time of trouble?

—JOB 38:22

Chapter Twenty-One

When Angel was about six years old, school officials began to insist she attend school. This is something Dr. Heinrich had put a stop to a few years earlier. He told officials Angel was in his care and he would decide when the time was right for her to go to school.

Angel never enjoyed good health, but for a few years in the late 1970s, her health somewhat stabilized. Bill and Lily received exciting news from the doctor during that time: the leaking valve next to Angel's heart was no longer a problem, and surgery was no longer needed. Hence, the doctor agreed it might be time to start her education.

Angel was enrolled in a school for children with special needs called Town and Country. She was picked up every day in a specially equipped van or bus and returned in the afternoon. Angel couldn't have been happier. She enjoyed the other children immensely. Lily thought it would be a good opportunity for her, too, to do some volunteer work for Town and Country.

Lily saw a great many things at Town and Country—some good and some bad. She remembers a young man by the name of Kenny who lived at a home for the mentally handicapped called Springview. Kenny was brought into the lobby at Town and Country, and then he was abandoned for the most part. Kenny just sat there as other children played around him, until it was time for him to be taken back to the nursing home. Lily wanted to take him home, care for him, and give him a decent home. But caring for Angel was a full-time challenge, which is why Lily and Bill chose not to have any more children.

There was another young lady at Town and Country who would become very upset and even violent. She would twist her hands into the teachers' and other children's hair. The young lady was so unmanageable, the children and most of the staff were afraid of her. But Lily had no fear of the child. Instead, she showed a kindness and gentle compassion the child had probably never experienced. Lily felt a lack of affection was the only reason for the child's bad behavior. She also wondered how many of the children at Town and Country were enrolled there for no more reason than rejection and the absence of love. Doctors and staff at the facility were impressed with Lily's uncanny ability to manage certain so-called problem children. For this reason, they suggested Lily return to school and become a child psychologist.

It was nothing more than a kind heart and love for children that made Lily who she was. Lily had spent an entire lifetime with a child on her hip, and she has never lost one moment of compassion for children. Perhaps she would have been a good childcare professional. But she was happy to be Angel's mother and have the things, and the life, she had.

I'm proud to say I share Lily and Bill's love for children. I happen to believe that when the molding begins at infancy, there is an opportunity to shape a child into a good and respectable person. There was a time of innocence even for the worst of people. As Lily believed with the young girl at Town and Country, I believe a series of bad events is the reason for most bad behavior in people. Abuse or neglect, without a doubt, play a large part in what becomes of children. I don't believe a child becomes bad simply because of something the child did or did not do. Our children are the products of us as parents and our guidance.

How can a young man keep his way clear? By guarding it according to thy word.

—PSALMS 119:9

Chapter Twenty-Two

There could not have been a more perfect day. It was the last week in April, and Lily had taken Angel into the backyard, where they sat on a blanket beneath the fruit trees. Lily often took Angel outside on warm sunny days, but this day was exceptionally wonderful. The sky was deep blue and without a cloud. The birds were chirping, and there was a low hum from the bees. The trees were in full bloom, and there was little or no sound from the city.

Lily was having her usual conversation with Angel. The two of them had their own way of communicating. Lily took a look around and realized how blessed she was. Angel's health hadn't been a problem in recent years—at least not as bad as it had been in the beginning.

Lily had labored her entire life to get to where she was, and at that moment, she realized she had achieved a greater happiness than she had ever expected to find. She had a good husband, a nice home, and Angel Rose. They were accustomed to earning things the hard way and struggling to hang on to them. She had never had so much to be thankful for—but how long could this good fortune last?

Lily then began to have dark and foreboding thoughts of the possibilities. She began to wonder, what if something were to happen to Bill? What on earth would she and Angel do without Bill? Or how would Bill and Angel survive without her? The most troubling question of all was how the two of them could go on without Angel.

Lily forced herself to snap out of it and come to the realization that this day was what she should be thankful for. The serenity of being there in her backyard, in this beautiful setting she and Bill had created with their own hands, watching her daughter play. That's what was important for now, not some unforeseen mishap that had not yet happened. There could be dark and dreadful events in the future, but nothing could erase these memories, for this was what she had dreamed of all of her life.

• • • •

Angel began to walk at the age of six. It wasn't much more than just a step here and a step there, yet it was very exciting. Lily and Eloise would take her into the backyard and stand her up along the chain-link fence. Using the fence for support, Angel would walk from one end of the fence to the other. Eventually, Angel started to take steps on her own. In fact, she would meet her Ya-Ya (Dad) at the door.

Another of Angel's proud accomplishments was when she learned to hold her own drink cup. No one knows just why, but shortly after she was enrolled at Town and Country, Angel refused a cup when Lily offered it to her. She almost acted as if she was afraid of it. We can only speculate, but perhaps someone accidently spilled something on Angel at school, whether hot or cold, and she never forgot it. Angel never forgot anything.

For instance, once when Angel was younger, Lily caught her trying to put something into the electrical outlet. She tapped the back of Angel's hand and scolded, "No, Angel—hot." Angel never forgot that lesson, and she was careful to stay clear of outlets and anything hot from that day on. Lily was allowed to cook on the kitchen stove, but Bill wasn't allowed near it. Angel was afraid Ya-Ya would get burned, and she would exclaim, "No—hot!"

It was at about this age that Angel went to see a dentist in Columbus. Angel had nice teeth, although doctors were concerned her teeth and gums might be affected by the many medications she was forced to take. Angel didn't cooperate at the dentist. Several methods were used, including restraint and laughing gas, but they were unable to treat her.

Perhaps it was a reaction to her other medications, but shortly after leaving the dentist, Angel fell into some kind of arrest. Lily and Angel were riding in the back seat, and Bill was driving on the busy interstate. Bill's first reaction when Lily screamed was to turn around and head back toward Columbus for help, but there was no place whatsoever to turn around.

For long, terrifying moments, Lily fought to revive Angel. Angel was completely limp, and she was not breathing. For all means of description, Angel was dead, but Lily continued to work with her. Finally there was a slight groan, and she began to breathe again.

Through the years, there were other frightening moments such as this. Lily and Bill were always on the alert for the slightest irregular sound from Angel's bedroom. Twenty-four hours a day, they worried and they watched for any signs of trouble.

What tormented them most were the seizures. As she grew immune to each antiseizure medicine, Angel would have debilitating attacks. The doctors would then introduce her to a new medication, but Angel would suffer seizures until it could take effect.

Each and every seizure left Angel weaker and more debilitated. When she would awaken from a seizure, she would be completely exhausted. For a short time after, she would appear limp and lethargic. The seizures continued to chip away at her health, both physically and mentally. Then one day, the decision was made to take her out of school. This was a painful decision for a number of reasons, but Lily, Bill, and Dr. Heinrich had discussed it at length. The decision was unanimous. Angel had become too sick to attend school. The fear was that Angel would suffer a seizure at a moment when she was unattended, fall, and hurt herself.

Angel loved going to school, and she had been learning things, at least in the beginning. Sign language was one of her accomplishments. This was very important for Angel, as she was unable to communicate verbally.

Lily and Angel would both miss the people at Town and Country. They had met some wonderful and extraordinary people there. It takes a special kind of person to care for children such as Angel, and there were lots of them at Town and Country. As a whole, they were wonderful people teaching wonderful children.

Let not many of you become teachers, for you know that we who teach shall be judged with greater strictness.

—2 JAMES 3:1

Chapter Twenty-Three

Angel's sicknesses eventually robbed her of her ability to walk, then to stand, and then one day she was unable to crawl. It seemed Angel was becoming weaker each day. Through a series of blood studies, Dr. French discovered Angel was anemic. For this condition, he prescribed iron, but Angel would have no part of it.

Lily asked the doctor if it would be helpful to give Angel a vitamin-enriched drink called Ensure. The doctor agreed it would be very helpful. Lily began giving her the drink, and she regained some strength. However, Angel never had an appetite for anything. I believe because she was forced to take so many medicines, she imagined everything would have a bad taste. It is sadly true she had to endure the most bitter and foul-tasting medicines in existence. But these, of course, were the only things that kept her alive.

Throughout her lifetime, Angel was fed small amounts of food with a spoon. She was never able to eat solid foods; her food couldn't have a consistency thicker than pudding. I couldn't begin to count the number of times I called Lily and asked, "What are you up to?" and she would reply, "Oh, I'm just trying to get Angel to eat." That was a feat that could sometimes take hours to complete.

Angel suffered chronic kidney infection as a result of reflux from bladder fluids into her kidneys. Dr. Parsons was the kidney specialist who searched for answers to the ever-changing questions, as many different medicines were used to treat the condition. Over the years, there were so many antibacterial and antibiotic medicines, Lily couldn't remember them all.

How many times Lily and Bill watched the tubes and watched the needles piercing Angel's little arms. How many times they watched as her fingers were pricked for blood samples and bitter medicines were poured into her. These events are too numerous to count, but Angel was always well behaved, and she cooperated with every treatment.

If, however, the pain became too much to endure, she would cry and try to pull away. Lily would then ask for a little time in private with her. She would take Angel to a quiet place and talk to her. As Lily put it, she would tell her little baby stories and whisper soft words of encouragement. Angel would then calm down and cooperate with the treatment. She never complained—she just did what Momma asked of her. For this reason, doctors and nurses enjoyed treating Angel.

• • • •

On the first day of June 1984, Lily received a disturbing phone call. Mrs. Heinrich said, "Mrs. Skiles, I'm calling to inform you that my husband, Dr. Heinrich, is retiring from the practice of medicine."

This was devastating news to Lily and Bill. What would they do without their beloved Dr. Heinrich? There were lots of other doctors, but there was only one Dr. Heinrich.

Lots of memories passed through Lily's mind as she tried to think of a way to break the news to Bill. She remembered when

Dr. Heinrich called to have her check Angel's vital signs and then would call every fifteen minutes until he knew Angel had stabilized. She remembered when Angel was six and very sick with a temperature well over 100. The hospital staff was preparing to restrain her and place an IV tube into her arm. Dr. Heinrich demanded Lily be given a chance to get Angel to drink. He said, "Restraint is the very last option, and I won't allow it until all else has failed." Little by little, just a few drops at a time, Lily was able to get Angel to drink milk and juice until she was rehydrated enough that the IV was no longer necessary.

Mrs. Heinrich said that in the future Dr. Heinrich's patients would be seen by Dr. Corral. They took Angel to see Dr. Corral, but they were unimpressed for some reason. Lily couldn't quite put her finger on it, but there was something in Dr. Corral's demeanor she and Bill didn't approve of. Perhaps they were looking for the same high standards and compassion they had come to know with Dr. Heinrich. He was not going to be easy to replace, for he had been there through it all. With Lily's pregnancy, Angel's dangerously high body temperatures, the seizures, as well as her good accomplishments, Dr. Heinrich had been there. He must have been quite pleased with all the accomplishments from this child most physicians thought wouldn't survive her first day of life.

There's no question about it: without Dr. Heinrich, Angel would not have lived. How many times he was called upon in the middle of the night, and he never failed to answer. The doctor would see Angel at all hours of the day, just as Lily and Bill monitored her condition around the clock. Lily would put Angel to bed at about 10:00 p.m. and everything would seem completely normal, and then three or four hours later, she could be burning up with a fever.

Yes, Dr. Heinrich was a tough act to follow, and they just didn't think that Dr. Corral was the right choice. There would be a number of doctors who would try to help, as Angel's quest for life was just beginning.

The next was Dr. French, who had discovered Angel was anemic. He was a good and caring doctor with an office on the north side of town, not far from where Dr. Heinrich's office had been. However, like Dr. Heinrich, Dr. French was aging and would soon retire from medicine. This worried Lily and Bill, after just losing their first doctor.

Their concerns became reality one day in the late 1980s when Dr. French suffered a massive heart attack while at work in his office. The *Springfield News-Sun* reported that the only thing that saved Dr. French's life was the fact that Dr. Dahdah, a renowned cardiologist, had an office in the same building. He was no doubt responsible for saving the doctor's life.

Dr. French was the Skiles family doctor for about six years, and then he, too, retired in 1990. There were several short-term doctors after that. There were Drs. Mong and Quok, both of whom were good, but they belonged to a type of medical organization that required them to go elsewhere when asked. Dr. Quok had been Angel's doctor for about two years when he was transferred to a hospital in Charleston, West Virginia. Dr. Mong treated Angel for almost three years before being sent to Riverside Hospital in Cincinnati. There were a couple of others until they found Dr. Venkatesh, a young and reputable doctor who remained Angel's doctor for the rest of her life.

Finding and keeping a family doctor was only part the challenge. There were lots of well-qualified physicians; the problem was finding doctors with the passionate drive to treat someone as sick as Angel. Many doctors were unwilling to take on such an enormous responsibility, while others simply didn't think it was possible to keep her alive. At almost any given time, she required a team of specialists. There were cardiologists, urologists, neurologists, ear-nose-and-throat specialists, and others.

Lily and Bill had learned through the years that doctors are as prone to human frailty and doubt as anyone. When they noticed some sign of weakness in the medical staff, they immediately moved on.

To them, Angel wasn't just another sick person; she was their little girl. Angel was their daughter, whom they had brought into the world to love and care for unconditionally. They had watched her grow, play, and enjoy life. They knew Angel's life would probably be cut short, but they were determined to keep her as long as they possibly could. And this meant giving her the best medical care available. They also knew Angel was a fighter, and that given a chance, she would outlive all the doctors' expectations.

Heal me, O lord and I shall be healed; save me, and I shall be saved; for thou art my praise.

—2 JEREMIAH 17:14

Chapter Twenty-Four

My wife and I moved back to Springfield when I left military service in the spring of 1980. We had two children: Nikki was six years old, and Jeremy was three. My children loved Angel Rose and vice versa. Jeremy was the hyper one in those days. He used to run circles around Angel, and she would laugh until she cried. Jeremy enjoyed entertaining Angel, and she knew there was going to be fun and excitement whenever he came to visit. Of all his cousins, Jeremy enjoyed Angel the most. He always liked to show off and be the clown. The two of them used to play for hours on end. But even when he was older and his playful energy faded away, Jeremy and Angel's love for one another remained.

In 2000, Jeremy's son Bradley was born. He now became Angel's playmate until he, too, became older and lost that same interest in playing. After skipping a few years, Jeremy's son Caden was born in 2008. He would become Angel's little playmate for the remainder of her life.

· · · ·

It was on the first full day of summer 1983 that our father passed away. The last six years of his life were spent in and out of hospitals. He had suffered chronic artery disease and had undergone numerous surgeries, including two amputations. His right lower leg had to be removed just below the knee when blood circulation had failed. A short time later, the remaining portion above the knee had to be amputated as well. This operation resulted in a blood clot that passed through his heart, causing a heart attack. Although he would live for some time after the attack, he would not be strong enough for prosthesis.

He knew he was slowly dying, and one day he said to me, "I've selected my burial site, and I want you to build a cover over my grave." He did not want any rain or snow to fall on his grave, so he described to me what he wanted. I drew it up and showed it to him. He looked it over and nodded slowly in approval. He reiterated that he did not want any rain or snow to fall on his grave.

After he passed, I asked the funeral directors if they would leave the tent over the grave long enough for me to build the cover, and they granted me three days beyond the burial. First the materials had to be found, purchased, and hauled in. I remember being very tired, but my brothers were helping, and the work continued. We were working feverishly, but we were running out of time. On the morning of our last day of construction, we removed the tent while we worked. The grave was exposed during this time. I wasn't worried, for I knew we would be finished by day's end. More importantly, we were in the middle of a drought—there hadn't been rain for weeks.

First we placed the bricks, and then we installed a four-sided hip-type roof. But as we nailed the final shingle, a jet-black cloud appeared over the mountaintop. Out came a downpour that lasted about twenty minutes, and then the drought continued for days. Not a drop of rain ever fell on our dad's grave, and I couldn't help believing the short downpour was a sign of divine approval.

I'm about to go the way of all the earth. Be strong and show yourself a man.

—1 KINGS 2:2

Chapter Twenty-Five

Over the years, Lily and Bill had learned to improvise in a number of ways. They couldn't afford to eat out, not even at fast food restaurants. So Lily learned to make restaurant foods at home. She made McDonald's, Kentucky Fried Chicken, Burger King, and others. As you can imagine, the meals were not exact replicas, but they were certainly close enough.

Another improvisation was when they often had frozen TV dinners, Lily saved all the empty trays. She then used the trays to package other leftovers and freeze them. When the frozen meals were cooked in the microwave for a few minutes, the food tasted as fresh as when it was first cooked.

Lily has always been an excellent cook, whether she cooked hotdogs or large meals for family gatherings. Angel's birthday party was an occasion we all enjoyed. It was happy and festive with lots of food, cake, and balloons. It was an event my family and Bill's family looked forward to. My son, Jeremy, expected Lily to also bake a birthday cake for him every year on the fifth day of June.

• • • •

In the summer of 1981, Bill received some rough-cut oak two-by-fours and heavy-duty sheet metal Robbins & Myers had intended to throw away. I had a little knowledge in the construction industry, so Bill and I decided to construct a storage shed in the back corner of the yard. Bill needed a place to store things such as lawn chairs, the lawn mower, and the tiller. The only place for storing such things was a small closet-like area with a door that opened out to the driveway.

The lumber was heavy, full of splinters, and hard as a rock. In order to cut the sheet metal, we turned the blade backward on a seven-inch circular saw. Cutting the sheet metal created a horrendous racket that reverberated throughout the neighborhood. The shed was only about eight feet wide and twelve feet long, and we worked on it every day after work.

Finally after three or four days of hammering and sawing, the shed was finished. The sheet metal had a prefinished, baked-on gray paint, and when it was complete, Bill's shed was as nice and functional as any in the neighborhood. What Bill and I were the most proud of was the fact that we built it from material that probably would have just been thrown away.

I worked as a contractor throughout the 1980s, and if Bill's hours were cut short or he was laid off, he would work with me. Bill and I had a lot of fun working together. He never seemed to get tired. I always took my time, sipping on a soft drink and working at my own pace. Bill, on the other hand, never stopped—he would work straight through. Whether it was hot or cold outside, he just kept on working.

I used to say to him, "Bill, why don't you take a break, get something to drink, and rest for a while?"

He would just say, "Nope, I'm okay."

Then when we finally took a break, he would quickly guzzle down some water or a pop and say, "Well, I'm ready. Let's hit it again."

Most of my workers were younger and constantly complained

or needed guidance. Bill wasn't that way, and I suppose that's the reason I enjoyed working with him. Bill and I talked quite a bit as we worked, but not about work. We had known each other for a number of years by then. We never needed to discuss who had to do what next with a project—it just seemed to come naturally.

Then in early spring 1985, Bill and Lily's thirteen-year-old furnace failed. The company hired to replace it also offered a discount on a central air conditioner. After twelve summers in the home, they could now sleep in comfort during the hot season. And the maple tree in front was now large enough to provide morning shade in the front of the house.

There was a small concrete slab in front of the back door, and in 1978, Bill and his brother Larry expanded it into a large sixteen-by-twenty-two patio. While some families considered Northern Estates as temporary starter homes, Lily and Bill slowly transformed theirs into a moderate and comfortable home for life.

With the new air conditioner, large patio, storage shed, and a beautiful shade tree, what more could there possibly be? Simple answer: Lily had always longed for a front porch.

I was almost finished building my first home, when one day she said to me, "Do you think it would be possible to build a porch onto the front of our house?"

I answered with, "Sure. Why wouldn't it be possible?"

Bill then said, "Well, I don't think the city would allow it, because there has to be at least thirty feet from the curb to the foundation in front."

I said, "Then we'll ask the city for a variance. We'll tell the city planning commission that Angel has to have a porch."

Lily was so skeptical and worried there would be problems acquiring permission from the city. She would say, "I just know they're not going to allow us to build it. I just know it."

I would reassure her, "Lily, it might take a little time, but we'll get the permit." I couldn't remember her as impatient about anything as she was during the building of that porch. That was spring of 1986, and I suppose she wanted the porch in time for summer.

As good fortune would have it, the decision Bill and Lily had made years before to choose a dining room versus a garage proved to be another advantage. Every house within blocks had been built with a garage. The fact that their house had not meant it was positioned differently on the lot. Hence, the setback was forty feet to the foundation, giving us the distance needed. I drew up a somewhat rudimentary sketch, Bill and I presented it to the city building inspector, and we had our permit.

A good friend of mine by the name of David Jones was helping me build my own house, and he helped with the porch project. Bill helped when he could, but he was working a lot of overtime. David and I dug the hole for the footings, and we hired a concrete contractor to finish the floor and foundation. David and I then completed the roof and the soffit and placed indoor-outdoor carpet on the floor.

Lily and Bill hung a swing on their new porch, and Angel was in heaven. This became known as her "ming-ming," and no one messed with her ming-ming. Angel would spend hours in her swing, and it was rewarding to know I had helped create something she enjoyed so.

I kept my heart from no pleasure, for my heart found pleasure in my toil, and this was my reward for my toil.
                                        —ECCLESIASTES 2:10

Chapter Twenty-Six

When she was just a baby, Angel discovered her love for water. They used to take her to Clark Lake on weekends and dangle her feet in the water. Lily says that if they would have let her go, she probably would have swam away.

Angel had many loves. She had her favorite TV shows, such as *Sesame Street* and *The Muppets*. She had a passion for music. She loved country and bluegrass just like her mom, but Angel enjoyed any kind of music. Her music could be heard throughout the day, and she would become upset if anyone turned it down or off. This was not to say she would throw a tantrum like other children. Angel was a tenderhearted child, and if she was disappointed or if she hurt herself, she would only cry.

• • • •

Angel loved being around people. She was always happy and bubbly in a crowd. Lily and Bill would take her to the Clark County Fair every year. Those visits were some of the most joyous occasions of her life. The man who operated the carousel would recognize Angel, and he would stop the other children and say, "Hold it—Angel goes on first."

Once they took her to Kings Island, a large amusement park just north of Cincinnati. Bill placed her into a tiny car and let her drive it around with the other children. She loved anything that resembled a car or had a motor. Angel would pretend she was driving a car just like Momma and her Ya-Ya.

When she was about thirteen years old, Angel had outgrown the type of toys little children like to ride or push around, but she was unable to ride a bicycle or even a tricycle. After a frustrating search for something suitable, Bill decided to build a toy she could sit in or push around. So he built her a little car, complete with four wheels and a steering wheel. It was about five feet long, and Lily upholstered the seat and dash. Angel spent a lot of time in her car. She used to sit in her car and watch Ob (Bob) mowing the grass next door.

Angel was always fascinated with anything that had a motor. She used to like sitting on the front porch at their getaway home in Kentucky and watching the other children as they rode their all-terrain vehicles or dirt bikes on the road in front of the house. Our mother used to say that if not for Angel's physical inability, she would have probably driven away on a motorcycle.

• • • •

Angel enjoyed church services, but when she was a little girl, the seizures became so frequent, they had to stop taking her to church. However, Lily and Bill made sure she received religious sustenance. She was taught to love Jesus, and when Bill was at work, Lily and Angel would listen to gospel music until she was ready for bed. They placed a picture of the Good Shepherd above Angel's bed as a reminder that Jesus was watching over her.

And consider this day (since I am not speaking to your children who have not known or seen it), consider the discipline of the lord your God, his greatness, his mighty hand and his outstretched arm.

—DEUTERONOMY 11:2

Chapter Twenty-Seven

On a Sunday afternoon in the summer of 1986, Lily, Bill, and Angel went out for a drive. They were headed west on Columbus Avenue when Lily saw a sign that read "Free puppy." It was so spontaneous when Lily asked Bill to stop, he thought she was joking. It was a little unusual because they had never been, as they say, "pet people." In fact, they had never even discussed getting a pet.

Bill waited in the car with Angel as Lily went to the door. A middle-aged Asian lady with very broken English answered.

Lily said, "Do you still have the puppy?" and the lady responded, "Yes—free."

The lady then led Lily down into a very poorly lit basement. Lily was still a little blind from the bright day outside. She couldn't see much, but she heard the dog whimper. As she reached the bottom of the steps, the puppy came running out. The puppy had been sleeping in what had once been a coal bin.

It was a male dog, but it was hard to say what breed it was or even what color. One thing was certain: the puppy was completely covered with fleas, and he was in very poor health.

In spite of all that, they rushed him home, bathed him, fed him, and groomed him. Lily treated him for the fleas and then wrapped him in a towel. The dog became completely quiet, so Lily asked Bill to check on him, for fear he had died. He wasn't dead—he was sleeping soundly, probably for the first time in his short life.

In no time at all, the dog became a part of them. He was now healthy and had that nonstop energy that demands, "Come on and play with me." They named him Fluffy, and if you saw him, you'd know why. He was stark white with hair long enough to touch the ground. The only part of him that wasn't white was his shining black nose.

My son loved that little dog, and between Jeremy and Fluffy, they kept Angel pretty well occupied. Angel had long, beautiful hair that hung to her knees. Lily would braid it, and Fluffy would run circles around Angel, nipping at her braid, as she sat on the floor or on a blanket outside. One day the puppy was tugging just a little too hard at her hair. As he ran past her, Angel caught his back leg. Holding him up to Lily, she exclaimed, "Momma?"

Fluffy never left Angel's side. When he was completely exhausted from hours of playing, he would lay sleeping at her feet. Fluffy didn't allow anything to get near Angel without his approval. The fenced-in backyard was Angel and Fluffy's domain, and neither a bird nor squirrel was allowed to encroach. Fluffy didn't like being indoors, unless it was storming. He would come in only if Lily commanded him to, and as soon as a storm abated, he was at the door, begging to go out again.

In 2001, Fluffy began to suffer seizures. He was now fifteen years old, and age was catching up with him. Soon after the seizures began, he became less and less active, until finally he was almost unable to stand. Then, finally, he stopped eating. It was painfully obvious Fluffy was doomed, and he appeared to be consigning himself to his fate.

Lily thought if she could get him to eat, he would surely feel better. So she went to Fluffy, and after pleading with him, he obediently ate two small bites. They knew little could be done for him, and his trip to the vet would probably be one way.

Fluffy never liked riding in a car, but on this day in 2002, he was completely calm when Bill placed him in the car to take him to the vet. Lily said he looked almost childlike as he sat in the passenger's seat when Bill drove away with him. There was nothing that could be done for their old friend, and a short time later, Bill returned with only the leash.

Sixteen years of happy memories ended that day, and a part of them was gone. The pain of losing Fluffy was so devastating, they swore to each other they would never have another pet.

Apparently, Angel missed Fluffy more than we realized. Years later, there was a small dog in the neighbor's yard, and she would insist on being taken outside to hear the doggie bark. Angel loved to hear him bark, and she liked to watch him run along the fence. To her, it was like watching a child playing, and it made her happy.

The poor man had nothing but a little ewe lamb, which he had bought. And he brought it up, and it grew up with him and with his children; it used to eat of his morsel and drink from his cup, and lie in his bosom, and it was like a daughter to him.

—2 SAMUEL 12:4

Chapter Twenty-Eight

Bill's father, John Skiles, was a fascinating fellow. When he was seventy years old, he could jump flatfooted over a four-foot fence. When he got together with his sons, you'd swear he was their brother instead of their dad.

John was always happy and smiling. He never seemed to know a dull moment. John had remained single after Bill's mom died. When Sadie passed away in 1953, John had a tombstone placed on her grave with his name next to hers, so he could join her when his time came.

But life was becoming lonely for the old coal miner. After many years of being a bachelor, John finally married a widow by the name of Vernie Mullet. John and Vernie had only been married a few years when on August 14, 1986, Bill received the news that John was gravely ill. Without symptoms or warning signs, John had suffered an aneurysm.

John was in Weeksbury at the time, so he was rushed to McDowell Hospital. It was thought to have been a miracle that John had lived long enough to reach the hospital. John stabilized, but the prognosis was grim. After about two weeks in the hospital, John was moved to a nursing home, where he passed away on September 11.

Just before her death, Sadie had made John and the other children promise to take care of Bill, as he was the baby of the family.

It seemed oddly appropriate that John was buried on Bill's birthday, September 16, next to Sadie in the Johnson Family Cemetery. It was a large funeral procession, as John Skiles had been loved and respected by many throughout Kentucky, Tennessee, and Ohio. John was eulogized with lots of fond memories and wonderful words, but the most meaningful was that he was a good father. John Skiles was seventy-nine years old.

In life and in death they were not divided; they were swifter than eagles, they were stronger than lions.

—2 SAMUEL 1:23

Chapter Twenty-Nine

On a Friday afternoon in the late 1980s, Lily sat on a blanket with Angel in the backyard. It was a warm, sunny day, and the smell of the grass clippings pervaded the air. Bill had mowed the day before, and the yard looked pruned and well coifed. These were the quiet times she enjoyed with her daughter. She had completed the morning chores and was now contemplating what had to be done next. The house was clean and in order, Angel had been fed and bathed—perhaps she had some free time after all.

It was then a car pulled into the driveway that she didn't recognize. When the driver got out, she realized it was Sandy Cornez from Town and Country School. Sandy had been Angel's teacher. Sandy was petite and, as they say, "cute as a button" with a round face and chestnut-brown hair. She and Lily had become very close friends over the years. Their common bond had always been their unconditional love for children.

Everyone should have the good fortune to know someone like Sandy Cornez. Lily always described her as feisty or sassy. The children at the school were her children, and she let no one get in the way of that. Whenever they took the children for an outing or a field trip, Sandy would say to others who were waiting in line, "You'll have to wait. My children go first." Sandy truly loved those children.

There was only one fundamental difference Lily and Sandy had to mutually accept. Lily didn't know about that difference until the day she asked for Sandy's address because she wanted to send her a Christmas card. Sandy quite assertively said, "No, Lily, do not send me a Christmas card. I'm Jewish."

Sandy was smiling and waving vigorously as she came up the driveway, yet there was something troubling in her demeanor. There was something strange, and for the first time since they had known each other, Sandy didn't appear to have control of the situation. Before Lily could ask what was wrong, Sandy began to speak.

"Lily, I just had to stop and see you before I go. My husband is divorcing me for another woman, and I'm moving to Oregon."

"What?" Lily replied. "Sandy, I'm so sorry. What in the world is wrong with him—he must be crazy."

"I don't know, Lily," Sandy said. "He's just not happy, I guess. And sometimes the only choice is to move on. Our two sons are very upset about the whole thing. They just can't come to terms with the fact that after all these years, their parents are getting a divorce."

"But is there no chance for reconciliation?" Lily asked.

"No, I don't think so, Lily. It's much too late for that," she replied sadly.

Lily then said to her, "Sandy, you can't go. We need you here. What about the school—how can they go on without you?"

Sandy said, "Yes, I know what you're saying. It's not easy to leave. But you know, Lily, it's beginning to have a profound effect on me—this whole divorce thing. It's all taking a toll on me, and I guess I just need a new beginning. I'm sure I'll end up teaching in Oregon."

Lily didn't know what to say, so Sandy continued, "You know, Lily, I sometimes find myself crying in the night and thinking about those kids. There's just so much suffering and loss. You're seeing it with Angel, but I've had to endure the loss of a lot of kids over the years. I see them go through so much, and I'm unable to do anything about it. You and Bill are loving, caring parents who shelter and nurture your child. But that's not always the case with some parents. Many of those children are neglected or even abandoned. They're brought to the school and then taken right back to a nursing home or some foster care. They're not loved and cared for like Angel. Angel is one of the few fortunate ones."

Lily thought for a moment and then said, "Well, I remember Kenny. It seemed that he was abandoned. They brought him there, and then just left him until it was time to take him back to the nursing home."

Sandy lost all expression and became a little somber at the mention of Kenny. "Oh, yes. Kenny," she said. "Now there was a special one. His parents were disabled, too, you know. Apparently they were unable to care for him. But don't let Kenny fool you, Lily. He liked being left alone. He enjoyed watching the other children, but he didn't really enjoy interacting with them. We often joked that Kenny was a grumpy old man who just wanted to be left alone."

Sandy then leaned over, took Angel's hand, and said, "How've you been, Angel Rose?" Sandy then looked up at Lily and said, "She's worse, isn't she, Lily?"

Lily said, "Yes, she is physically worse than the last time you saw her, but she's improving mentally. Angel's a lot smarter than most people think, but you're right—she's lost a lot of the strength in her legs. She can no longer walk or even crawl."

Sandy then kissed Angel on the cheek and said, "I'll always love you, Angel." Sandy stood up, hugged Lily, and said, "I'm going to go now, before I become more emotional than I already am. I'll miss you, Lily, and I'll call you as soon as I get settled in."

They were both beginning to well up as Sandy turned away. Lily never could stand endings and goodbyes. She felt like running after her to try convincing her not to go, to somehow undo whatever hurt she was suffering so things could be normal again.

Lily had spent countless hours alone while Bill was at work, and she didn't have a lot of friends as close as Sandy. She didn't work outside the home, and there was little opportunity to associate. Lily was tied to the home for the most part. This was not something she resented; it was just the way it was. Angel had to be cared for, and that required her presence at home.

Sandy and Lily wrote lots of letters over the years and talked on the phone quite a bit, but they remained long-distance friends. A few years after she moved away, Sandy came back for a visit. She stayed overnight with Lily and Bill, and the bond was as close as ever. Bill enjoyed Sandy as well. He, too, described her as feisty and sassy. He found her to be an interesting person and laughed joyfully at the mention of her. "Yeah, we liked Sandy a lot," he said to me.

We used to hold sweet converse together; within God's house we walked in fellowship.

—Psalms 55:14

Chapter Thirty

Angel turned eighteen on May 2, 1990. Although life for her was never easy, this was a period when she avoided the long hospital stays. There was, however, the constant threat of extreme body temperatures and tract infections. There were occasional cases of pneumonia with sore throat and cough, but these were symptoms Lily and Bill learned to deal with on a regular basis. The mere thought of pneumonia is enough to scare the wits out of most parents, but to Lily and Bill, it worried them the least.

Over the years, Lily and Bill became very light sleepers. They learned to keep themselves in somewhat of a twilight sleep, never allowing themselves to drift too deeply into slumber. They listened constantly for the slightest irregular sound or movement, for they knew catching and treating problems early was the only way to prevent severe sickness.

Angel was happy and for the most part healthy on her eighteenth birthday. Turning eighteen for Angel wasn't the traditional celebration it is for most children who are just about to enter adulthood. There were no proms, no learning to drive, no graduation ceremonies or plans for college. Year after year, Angel simply fought to stay alive.

Still, birthdays and other holidays were always fun around the Skiles home. They always celebrated with Angel as if she were a little girl. There was a family gathering with lots of food, cake, and ice cream. Every holiday meant lots of food and family members around. Lily always enjoyed cooking large meals, and the more people who came to dinner, the more she enjoyed it.

• • • •

I was living in Omaha, Nebraska, in 1995 when I received word that Bill's brother Cleck had passed away. Cleck was the eldest of Bill's siblings and had played a large role in raising Bill. Cleck developed lung cancer that claimed his life rather suddenly at the age of sixty-six. As often mentioned in these pages, the closeness of the Skiles family made it hard for them to accept the fact that Cleck was gone. What made Cleck's death even more unexpected was that longevity seemed to be normal in the Skiles family.

Bill had always been a strong and positive force, but losing Cleck was really tough on him. I saw a side of Bill I had never experienced. We spoke for several hours, and he openly wept as he told me stories about being much younger than Cleck and looking up to him almost the same way a child looks up to a father. He told me stories about riding on Cleck's shoulders when he became too tired to walk. Other members of the Skiles family told similar stories. The tragic loss of Cleck was one of many heartaches to come. The Skiles family would suffer a number of similar losses in the years to come.

• • • •

In 1998, Bill and Lily added a room onto the patio Bill and Larry had installed years earlier. The addition was a three-season sunroom. Sunrooms are not usually climate controlled, as was the case with this addition. They are not heated in the winter nor cooled in the summer.

The walls were almost all glass with very little space in between windows. It was a handsome structure Lily soon decorated with a picnic table and padded lawn chairs. She even put some of her antique furniture in the room. The additional space came in handy. It gave them a lot more living space. It came in handy for family gatherings as well.

This soon became Angel's favorite place in the whole world. From the time she woke up in the morning, that's where she wanted to be. Lily would turn on her music, and Angel would sit out in that room and play for hours. They used a small electric heater to take the chill out of the room when the weather was cold but still not too harsh.

By knowledge the rooms are filled with all precious and pleasant riches.

—PROVERBS 24:4

Chapter Thirty-One

On January 7, 2000, Lily, Bill, and Angel went shopping at Walmart. On the way home, Bill made a comment that it would have been his dad's birthday. They were just a couple of miles from home when Angel had a sudden attack. Her color changed, and she went completely limp. Lily was frantic—Angel wasn't breathing.

Just a few moments later, Bill pulled into the driveway. Angel was beginning to recover as Bill carried her into the house and placed her in her bed. As mentioned earlier, these attacks would completely drain the strength from her, so Angel fell asleep instantly.

Bill then turned his attention to Lily. She was pale, nauseous, and short of breath, and she was having chest pains. Lily just kept insisting Bill stay focused on Angel. Eloise came over to stay with Angel while Bill rushed Lily to Mercy Hospital.

The hospital staff didn't appear to be concerned at first. Lily just kept saying, "I have to go home. I have a sick child." Dr. Dahdah, the heart specialist who had saved Dr. French's life, was called in to perform a heart catheterization. He discovered Lily had suffered a mild stress-related heart attack.

Dr. Dahdah warned Lily about the amount of stress she was under, but what could she have done? Lily had cared for sick children throughout her life; therefore, stress was a part of her life. Lily remained in the hospital for the next three days, and that was the longest time she would ever spend away from Angel. Her recovery would be a long and slow process. For three months following the attack, Bill and Eloise took care of Angel until Lily recovered.

A heart attack at fifty-eight years old was enough to make Lily and Bill realize the dreadful day could come when they would no longer be able to keep Angel. This was something they didn't like to think about, but they knew it might someday become reality. They also knew that a child in a nursing home has a very short lifespan. Away from home, away from the people they love, most children fall into deep depression and die of broken hearts. The ultimate hope Lily and Bill would cling onto was that the three of them would fade away together.

Lily felt she should have a word with God regarding their situation. She asked that if the three of them were not to die together, then she would prefer Angel be taken first. They simply couldn't bear the thought of Angel dying a slow death in a nursing home. They knew that if not for the daily attention they had given her, Angel would not have survived.

Evening, and morning, and at noon, I will pray, and cry aloud: and he shall hear my voice.

—Psalm 55:17

Chapter Thirty-Two

For fourteen years, our brother Deanie had suffered a stomach ailment. He underwent a lot of surgery in 1986 and spent almost two months in the hospital. He seemed to do okay for a few years, but in late summer of 2000, his sickness recurred. For several weeks beginning in August, he was in and out of the hospital. I honestly believed he would get better. After all, he was only fifty-six years old. But Lily kept telling me I had better come home if I wanted to see him alive again.

I guess I didn't want to believe it, and we all knew Lily worried a lot. I had a sizeable company at that time, and it was a really bad time to go away. I called him at the hospital, and Deanie's biggest concern was when he would be allowed to go home. So I actually thought this was another episode that would pass, and I could see him in the winter when my work slowed down.

Deanie was a lot of fun. He was ten years older and somewhat of a hero to me when I was growing up. He and Lois had been married since 1967, and Lois was as dear to me as a sister could be. I remember coming home on leave from the military, and Lois would cook enormous meals. Then Deanie and I would stay up all night listening to his collection of classic country music.

I should have listened to Lily. I was working in northern Minnesota when the call came. It was October 4, 2000, when Eloise said, "Wynn, your brother has passed away."

It was about a five-hour drive to my home in Dayton, Minnesota. I packed quickly and booked a flight to Columbus, Ohio, the next day. I was held up in road construction and missed the first flight, so I was delayed about four hours. I got into Columbus just before sundown, grabbed a rental car, and drove to London to pick up my son, Jeremy. We stopped for dinner in Chillicothe and then drove until about midnight.

We kept seeing herds of deer along the roadside on US 23, and then near Louisa, we hit one. There were just too many to avoid. I hit the brakes, the car slid sideways, and we hit her just hard enough to knock her down. The deer got up, shook herself, and then walked away. We were lucky, and there wasn't much damage to the car. But it was enough to scare the daylights out of us, so we stopped for the night.

The wake was at my brother Ernie's church, and we made it just in time for the viewing. With all the racing and hurry to get to Weeksbury, it still hadn't hit me until that moment. Even with all the weeping and sorrow, I could not bring myself to believe my fifty-six-year-old brother was the man in that coffin. Deanie had a gentle soul and was a good father. He left behind a wife, five children, six brothers, six sisters, and a grieving mother.

My grief is beyond healing, my heart is sick within me.
                                                    —JEREMIAH 8:18

Chapter Thirty-Three

Our nephew was selling an almost-new mobile home in Shop Hollow, just across the road from our brother Ernie's house. It was already set up with all the necessary utilities. This would be perfect for Bill, Lily, and Angel. They could visit the family any time they liked and have a place to retreat at the end of the day. They bought the property in 2000, and right away they set out to make some changes.

Ernie loves projects, so the first thing he added was a small wooden deck just outside the back door. Lily then said to Ernie, "How can we make the master bedroom bigger?" and he said, "Well, you don't need all this closet space for your vacation visits, so let's remove these two closets."

Ernie made a lot of changes to the home. He created a larger bathroom and then added a covered porch in the front. Over the porch, he installed a corrugated tin roof and a ramp for Angel's wheelchair.

The home is tucked under the branches of a dense forest. The forest floor is covered with soft dark-green moss. Cool air flows from the forest, and at night when the windows are open, there's no need for air conditioning. Early-morning birds provide the wakeup call.

Several times I called Bill and Lily at their home-away-from-home, and when Bill answered, he would say, "I'm just sitting in the porch swing with Angel, listening to the rain on the roof." Angel loved the rain, and she loved watching the creek flow. Angel enjoyed the visits to Weeksbury. She would cheer and laugh when they arrived. That was about the only place she was ever comfortable away from home. However, in the later years, the trip was hard for her.

The front of the house faces east, overlooking the road and a cascading creek. Up the mountainside farther to the east and south is a view of the old pasture land. Up until fifty years ago, this had been grassy slopes kept clean and mowed short by livestock. It's easy for me to think back to the subtle clunking of a cowbell or the crowing of a rooster. There are still traces of the cow paths where we used to run and play as children.

There is still some of that nostalgic sentiment to be found there, although you might hear most people complain about the lack of Internet or poor cell phone reception. I guess modern times have found us, regardless of where we live. I personally believe we would be better off without a lot of the high-tech world. Some things are eternal—the mountains and the creek— at least in terms of the short lifespan of humankind. I guess I was more than a little complacent to the many wonderful sights and sounds of this area when I was a kid growing up there. But I've also known a lot of urbanites who would give anything to have a creek flowing past their front yard and these beautiful mountains in the fore and background.

By wisdom a house is built, and by understanding it is established.

—PROVERBS 24:3

Chapter Thirty-Four

It was a bright and sunny day in central Ohio, and Lily wanted to go shopping in Xenia. It was such a nice day, so they decided all three of them would go. Bill was driving while Lily and Angel sat in the back seat. Just north of Yellow Springs, they met a large number of motorcycles headed north. Angel liked motorcycles, and as Bill was pointing them out to her, he didn't see the car stopped in the road ahead, waiting to turn left. Bill slammed full force into the back of the car.

It was like an explosion happened inside the car, as any object not attached went flying, including Lily and Angel. Lily went face-first into the front seat, and Angel crumpled into the floorboard.

For a few moments, Lily and Angel were unconscious when Bill jumped out to check on them. His first reaction was to get Angel off the floorboard and find out how badly she was hurt. A man then came running to the scene and advised Bill not to move her. Lily was now able to speak, and her only concern was for Angel. Angel's mouth was bleeding, but aside from that, she was just mad because they wouldn't let her get off that floorboard.

An ambulance took Lily and Angel to the hospital, where they were X-rayed, treated for minor injuries, and released. Bill was cited on a charge of failing to control a motor vehicle and had to appear in court. However, as Bill had no history of traffic violations, all charges were dropped. Once more, they felt blessed, for this accident could have turned out much worse than it did.

· · · ·

In 2004, Lily and Bill decided they had to make some changes. In the earlier years, Angel had some strength in her legs. She could help a little when they needed to stand her up or get her into her wheelchair. Years of sickness had taken away that ability, and now Angel was almost completely limp. It took a lot of physical effort for Bill and Lily to maneuver her, and Lily insisted it was never a burden.

But they were getting older, and Angel was becoming more difficult to lift. They feared the day when they could no longer care for Angel. They knew it might someday come, but all they could do was take life one day at a time, for they had no intention of living without Angel.

The first thing they did was buy a van and had some special equipment installed to help get Angel in and out of the vehicle. The next thing was to install an overhead rail system with a harness-like seat in the house. This system is known as a barrier lift. They had to make a lot of changes inside the house in order for the system to work. First, they had to anchor the rail directly to the ceiling joists or rafters. Next, they had to remove the interior doors and replace them with pocket doors. Pocket doors slide into a cavity in the interior walls rather than swing on hinges. They installed the rail system in every necessary room in the house, except the new addition, which did not have the structural support needed for the lift. They also installed what is known as a Hoyer lift.

With the specially equipped van and the lift systems in the house, Lily and Bill could continue caring for Angel at home for a long time to come. The new equipment made things so much easier. During the course of the day, every piece of this special equipment was utilized. Each and every day, the Hoyer lift got Angel in and out of the tub, into bed, or into her wheelchair. The overhead system helped move her throughout the house.

• • • •

Sixteen inches of snow fell just after Christmas 2004, followed by a torrential downpour. The weight of the melting snow was too much for the sunroom, and the roof collapsed. Sadly, the contractor who built the room had made mistakes. The roof had been almost completely flat, with hardly any drainage tilt whatsoever.

Angel was lost without her playroom. Lily and Bill were saddened and frustrated by the loss as well. The room and much of what they had in it was a total loss. The insurance company would pay for some of the lost furnishings, and they wanted to pay the original contractor to replace the room. But if they rebuilt the sunroom the same as before, who was to say it wouldn't collapse under the next heavy snow?

I advised Lily not to let them rebuild the room with the same flat-roof design. I suggested footings, framed walls, and a strong raftered roof that would slope from the tallest point of the house. This would create proper strength as well as drainage pitch. But when Bill described my suggestion to the original contractor, they told him it wasn't possible. I recommended a couple contractors I had known when I was living in Ohio, but no one responded to their phone calls. Some other contractors came out and looked at the project but showed no interest in doing the work.

Work is usually slow for me in January, and after talking to Lily and Bill, I thought I might be able to help. On January 10, 2005, I headed out to Ohio to rebuild their collapsed room. My son, Jeremy, lived about fifteen miles from Lily, and he helped me in his spare time.

I drew up some plans, and Bill and I presented it to the city for a permit. Inches upon inches of rain had been falling during this time, and the building inspector didn't think we'd be able to dig or pour the footings. Surprisingly, we had no problems, and we actually increased the size of the room to create a three-directional view to the east, south, and west. We installed low-E windows and patio door, and the walls and ceiling were carefully insulated. We also installed a duct from the furnace and a gas fireplace, so the room could be heated and cooled for year-round use.

Angel was happy again, and now she could be in that room, regardless of the weather. The addition offers a great view of the sunrise and sunset, the same of course with the moon. Angel used to enjoy watching the changing phases of the moon. These were some of the simple little things that made her painful world worth living in. Even in her sickest moments, Angel found joy in life. Sometimes long before daylight and before the neighborhood would awaken, Angel would make Ya-Ya take her out into the new room to watch the brightening morning sky fade away the glow of a full moon. These were peaceful and memorable times for her.

What light through yon window breaks? Is it the East? Rise angry sun and kill the envious moon.
                                            —SHAKESPEARE, 1594

Chapter Thirty-Five

There are a lot of wonderful memories of Angel Rose. Although her body grew to about the size of a twelve-year-old child's, Angel's mind developed to that of a two-year-old's, or so the doctors say. While that may seem like the worst thing a parent could face, there's a way to see a silver lining: Lily and Bill were blessed with a child who was forever young and innocent.

Isn't there a little part in all of us that would love to keep our children young, innocent, and always with us? Babies are so much fun, as we love to watch them grow and develop their own personalities. But for most of us, we're a little saddened by the knowledge they will one day leave us.

After my two children became young adults, I had recurring dreams of them as babies. These dreams were so lucid, I could smell the baby powder. In my dreams, I would revisit long-ago memories of fun-filled days in the park, on vacation, or just a visit to the video store on a Friday evening. I would then awaken to the sad reality that time travel is impossible and I would never again see them in that stage of life.

The dreams continued throughout the latter part of the 1990s. They happened so frequently, I began to slip into a deep depression. I couldn't understand it, but at the same time, I was not going to use antidepressants to attempt to escape it. Just when I was nearing my breaking point, my grandchildren came along, and I realized I could create new and wonderful memories with them. This was perhaps what my subconscious mind was trying to tell me.

Lily and Bill had more than thirty-nine years of the memories I longed for. From the beginning to the end of her life, Angel lived absolute innocence. She never saw the bad things in people; she expected everyone to be as pure of thought as she was. Lily and Bill have a unique relationship as a couple. They've never been known to argue or fuss and fight; therefore, Angel was brought up in a peaceful and quiet home.

• • • •

Lily has always kept things neat, clean, and organized within their home. There was a lot of this in Angel as well. For instance, if there was a knickknack out of place as they passed through the house with her, she would have them stop so she could carefully put it back into place. She had a Golden Book about God that hung in her bedroom, and each night she would check to make sure it was hanging straight. If a throw rug was wrinkled, Angel would straighten it. She didn't like to wear shoes or socks in the house, so she would remove them the minute she entered the house and then arrange them neatly toe to toe.

Angel also kept her toys in place. She liked having two of everything. For instance, she had two small dollhouses that opened up. She called them "kitty-cat houses." When she was through playing with them, she would make sure they were closed and neatly put away.

• • • •

As Bill worked nights, Lily was the one who put Angel to bed and tucked her in. This consisted of two things. One was her night-night kiss, and then her last words for the evening had to be answered. Those words were "I love you."

Angel would play until she was completely exhausted, so when she was put to bed, she would usually fall asleep quickly. On one occasion, Lily was talking on the phone as she put Angel to bed, and she forgot the night-night kiss and the "I love you." Angel was extremely tired that night, and Lily thought she would fall asleep instantly. But instead, she turned and said, "Momma?" Lily then realized she had forgotten the important nightly ritual and how much it meant to Angel Rose.

All this might seem trivial to some parents, but to one who's lost a child, these little things are the most remembered. Lily was careful not to forget the little things that were so important to Angel. She remembered them from that day forward with Angel— and she'll remember them for the rest of her life.

Nights when Angel became restless in bed, Lily would tell her "little baby stories." The story consisted of three main characters: two "hop-hops" (rabbits) and Little Crow. The story was as follows:

> *Momma had cooked supper, and Ya-Ya had eaten it all and gone to work. Momma was washing the dishes when a storm came with lots of rain and rumbling thunder. During the storm, the two hop-hops came out and began to play in the puddles. Momma scolded from the window, "You hop-hops get out of the storm before I bust your tails!" The hop-hops then cried, "Oh no, we don't want our tails busted." Momma ran out into the rain to spank the two hop-hops, and they got scared and ran back into their house.*
>
> *Little Crow was watching the whole thing from a hollow tree and began to laugh. Little Crow had three friends. There*

was Mr. Redbird, Mrs. Mourning Dove, and Mrs. Robin.
Whenever Mr. Redbird saw Angel, he would sing, "Pretty,
pretty, pretty," and Mrs. Mourning Dove would ask, "Who,
who, who?" Then Mrs. Robin would answer, "Angel, Angel,
Angel."

Angel related very well with Little Crow. In fact, while sitting in her porch swing, she would caw loudly, and the crows would answer. Then in a very short time, the crows would gather in the maple tree in front of the house.

During those restless times, Lily would crawl into bed with Angel and tell her the little baby stories. However, the stories had to be word for word. If Lily told the story in a different way, made a mistake, or left out some little detail, then Angel would stop her and make her start the story from the beginning. Sometimes the stories had to be told twice, but when she had had enough, she would push Momma out of bed and then go to sleep.

She had an old knit blanket with a silk border. At night, she would run her fingers through the knitting and then fall asleep. We believe she formed this habit as a result of Lily holding her hand during all those episodes of sickness.

• • • •

Angel's love for water will never be forgotten. On the trip to Kentucky, they would cross the Ohio River at Ashland. On the way to Kentucky, Angel called the river "Rose's wa-wa" (water). Angel's middle name, Rose, was in honor of our youngest sister, Rose. Angel knew crossing the river into Kentucky meant a visit to Aunt Rose's house. On the way back home to Ohio, she called it "my wa-wa."

The US Army Corps of Engineers built a small waterfall below the spillway at the Clarence J. Brown Reservoir. They used to take Angel there and let her watch the water. She would always become happy and cheerful. She would sing and laugh as she imagined herself playing in the water.

• • • •

Angel loved taking a drive through the country to see the moo-cows. What fascinated her most were the calves in the spring. Whether human, animal, or just a doll, Angel loved babies. Angel's kind and gentle nature became even more apparent around babies. Her humble nature was without a doubt the inherited traits of many in her bloodline. These traits were from her mother, from our uncle Jim, our mother, and from every member of the Skiles family.

Our brother Jimmy and his wife, Maggie, had a couple horses. The fence ran along the lane in Shop Hollow, and Angel would make Bill stop so she could visit briefly with the horseys. Lily would save a few French fries, and when she fed them to the horses, they resembled cigarettes hanging from the horses' mouths. Angel thought it was hilarious.

• • • •

As mentioned, Angel was known for her ability to remember things. The three of them were out driving one day when a rude driver cut in front of Bill. Bill quietly mumbled, "Huh, must be a road hog." Bill didn't think Angel had heard him until she repeated what he said without the *h*. She simply said, "Og."

Sometime later while sitting in her ming-ming porch swing in Kentucky, my brother Ernie came to visit. He teasingly said to her, "Angel, I'm going to take your ming-ming."

Angel looked at him and said bluntly, "Og."

Hence, Ernie became known as "Og." Ernie was present as Angel lay on her deathbed. On several occasions during his visit, Angel mentioned "wa-wa." It could have been that she was thirsty, but Lily and Ernie are absolutely sure she was seeing a beautiful, clear, and gently flowing stream somewhere in the afterlife.

From the Heavens to the Earth doth soft raindrops fall. For those who giveth and those who taketh away.
—SHAKESPEARE, 1600

Chapter Thirty-Six

It must have been about twenty years ago that Walmart opened a store on the north side of Springfield. Lily became a shopper at this new and convenient location, and so did Angel.

Walmart became known as "Store-More," which was Angel's term for it. Store-More was a staple for Angel; it was a routine that had to be carried out daily. Angel knew Ya-Ya always left for work at 2:30 p.m., and if she didn't get her trip to Walmart, then she would proclaim, "Ya-Ya lie, lie, lie."

Angel's morning would begin with the phrase, "eat out of the house," which of course meant she wanted to eat out. Her first meal of the day would consist of a diet root beer, milk, and Boost (a vitamin-enriched drink). After that, it was a visit to Store-More. Sometimes they would shop at other stores such as K-Mart or the grocery store, but there was no substitute for Store-More.

Angel knew her way around Walmart, and she made Ya-Ya take her to certain features in her selected aisle. Of course she liked the toy aisles, but she also enjoyed the electronics with the large-screen TVs. But her favorite was the aquarium. She loved to see the fish swimming in the tank. The Walmart staff would always celebrate Angel's arrival. They were heard to say, "There's the man with the little girl in the wheelchair," and they would run to Angel.

Angel kept leading Bill to the end cap of a specific aisle. This happened repeatedly until one day Bill realized what she was so interested in. There was a display of Little Debbie snack cakes at the end of that aisle, and she wanted the small poster of Little Debbie. Lily and Bill found the store manager and asked if they could have the poster when the store was done with it. The manager said, "You know, Bill, we're going to be replacing that display, so I'm going to give that to Angel now."

Angel thought there was nothing in the world like it. Back at home, she positioned her small talking doll in a tiny chair and placed Little Debby in the doll's lap. When the doll talked, Angel would pretend Little Debby was doing the talking. She called her new toy "Woo-Woo," and she caressed it lovingly and whispered little secrets to it.

With the love Angel had for Woo-Woo, Lily and Bill realized she would be completely lost without it. They thought they'd better come up with a spare. They approached the Walmart store manager at the Portsmouth, Ohio, location. The manager simply smiled, took the poster from the shelf, and handed it to Bill. This was great, for now they could leave one at home and carry one on trips. Before the quest was over, they had acquired a third poster from another Walmart.

Angel had a small coffee table with drawers in her sunroom. She would sit on the floor next to it, place her doll and the Little Debbie poster on the floor next to her, and play for hours.

One time, Lily was concerned someone would step on the doll and break it, so she put it up on the table. A little later, Lily noticed the doll was back on the floor, so she placed it back on the table. Finally, Angel took the doll from the table and said quite frankly, "She'll fall." In other words, she didn't want her baby up on the table, where she could fall and hurt herself.

I thank thee, Father, Lord of heaven and earth, that thou hast hidden these things from the wise and understanding and revealed them to babes; yea, Father, for such was thy gracious will.

—LUKE 10:21

Chapter Thirty-Seven

From the time Angel was born, Lily made every stitch of Angel's clothes. She made pretty clothes Angel so loved to be dressed in. True to the nature of any little girl, she liked to show off her clothes. When they dressed her in the morning, she became to Lily "Momma's Baby," and to Bill she became "Ya-Ya's Doll."

Bill bought Lily a state-of-the-art sewing machine a few years ago. It was made by a Swedish company called Husqvarna. There were several versions of the machine, such as the Emerald and the Diamond. Lily's was the Topaz model. Lily has always loved sewing and quilting, and this thing was computerized. One of the benefits was that Husqvarna would send out a representative to help the customer set up and program the software.

The person who came to help Lily was a lady by the name of Helen. Lily couldn't seem to remember her last name, but she had seen her before at Jo-Ann Fabrics. Helen was a pleasant lady, middle aged with a medium build. She was very helpful, and they found they had a lot of things in common. People who do sewing and quilting seem to speak a language of their own.

After the setup was complete, they sat down at the dining room table for a soft drink. They talked about different stitching methods, quilts they had made, and how far the industry had come, especially with the new electronics in today's machines.

Throughout their visit, Lily kept noticing Helen watching Angel's every move. Lily finally said to her, "You seem to be fascinated with my daughter."

Helen took a deep breath and said, "Oh, you noticed. Well, I guess I should tell you, Lily, that I had a son like Angel. My husband and I divorced, and I was caring for him alone."

She continued, "I honestly thought I was the only person in the world with a mentally challenged child. His name was Bobby. My friends and even my closest relatives seemed to distance themselves from me after we found out Bobby was handicapped. I had never felt so alone. I struggled. Oh, let me tell you I struggled. Not just financially, but in every way you could imagine. I felt trapped in something I would never be able to escape."

She paused. "Do you mind telling me how old Angel is, Lily?"

Lily said, "She's thirty-five years old. Why do you ask?"

"I just wonder how you do it, Lily. How do you keep going day after day?"

Lily was beginning to feel a little uneasy at this point, and after a long pause, she said, "Well, Helen, it's not as bad as it probably appears. To begin with, I have a wonderful husband, who loves his daughter as much as I do. We have our problems, but we're a happy family, and we don't see Angel as a burden to us. We do things together, we enjoy life, and we consider every day to be a gift."

Lily then noticed tears beginning to well in Helen's eyes. Helen then slapped her hands to her knees and declared, "It's not fair. I tell you, it's just not fair. I struggled, and I kept my son for fourteen years, but I just couldn't hold on any longer. So I had him placed in a home. Sure, I had some freedom now, and I was beginning to date and live again."

Lily then asked, "How is Bobby doing, Helen?"

By this time, the woman was weeping as she responded, "Bobby? There is no Bobby. He died less than three months after I put him in that place."

Helen then rushed from the house and drove away.

About a year later, Lily saw Helen at a fabric shop. Lily tried to make conversation, but Helen didn't appear interested. Helen remained completely aloof as she gathered her things and hurried from the store. Lily and Bill never saw Helen again.

For I know my transgressions, and my sins are ever before me.

—PSALMS 51:3

Chapter Thirty-Eight

Lily and Bill had to cut a trip to Kentucky short and rush Angel back to Ohio for medical care. Dr. Venkatesh told them to take Angel directly to the emergency room.

When they arrived, a urine specimen revealed Angel had a urinary tract infection. The hospital staff did the testing and said it might be normal for Angel to have some infection. The staff didn't seem overly concerned about Angel's condition. They treated the infection with antibiotics and considered it a mild condition that would soon pass.

But throughout the fall of 2006, Angel was in and out of the doctor's office and the emergency room. Different medicines were administered, blood samples were tested, and cultures were grown; yet through it all, Angel's condition continued to deteriorate.

It's not my intention to underscore the efforts of caring and skillful doctors and nurses. We all know that without them, we would not have been able to keep Angel as long as we did. There was, however, a part of Angel's life only Lily and Bill experienced that medical staff just couldn't. Bill and Lily kept a baby monitor in Angel's room, and night after night, they remained awake to listen for warning signs. Angel slept in short naps with labored breathing, as if each breath could be her last. How many times they sat by her bedside, held her hand or patted away the sweat, and waited for some sign of improvement.

One problem doctors had was Angel's inability to tell them where she hurt. This made diagnosing and treating Angel's problems even harder. Angel had to be monitored around the clock. Even if she appeared to be okay, Lily would take her temperature and sometimes catch a rising temp before it could cause problems. Sometimes, though, mysteries baffled them and the finest of doctors.

On December 17, 2007, Lily heard a sound on the baby monitor that made her spring from bed and rush to Angel's side. Angel had a fever, and she was having trouble breathing. Lily called Bill at work and told him he would need to come home immediately. She then called Dr. Venkatesh.

When they arrived at the doctor's office, Angel was weak and had a temperature of 100. Lily told the doctor something would have to be done. Angel's constant fever, inability to breathe, and not sleeping were slowly killing all three of them.

Dr. Venkatesh said, "Well, we'll have to admit her for a couple days and do some extensive testing." From the time they left the doctor's office to their arrival at the hospital, Angel's temperature increased from 100 to 105.

The mere mention of a hospital stay brought back painful memories. Sights and sounds common in a hospital—these were etched into Lily and Bill, much like the lines on a phonograph record. Already they could hear the flow of the oxygen, the low beep of a monitor, and the garbled mumblings of the night staff. Across the hall a baby would cry or someone would moan. There, too, were the smells in their memory. The phenobarbital, the muscle rub, and the alcohol—it's all unforgettable to them.

With the amount of antibiotics and other drugs needed to fight the infection, a PICC line was prescribed. PICC stands for "peripherally inserted central catheter," and it's inserted into an artery in the right arm above the elbow and then pushed through the artery into the chest cavity.

After a couple of days of study, the doctors discovered Angel's prolonged kidney and tract infection had resulted in a condition known as sepsis. Sepsis is a form of blood poisoning that can be fatal if not treated in time. Powerful antibiotics such as Rocephin were administered directly into the bloodstream through the PICC line. Doctor Venkatesh added another warning regarding sepsis: once a person has been infected, they become even more susceptible to recurrence of the condition.

Angel was in critical condition for several days. The prescribed treatment for Angel's condition had been twenty-three days of hospitalization, but after nine days, the doctor allowed Angel to go home for the remainder of the holidays on the condition the PICC line remain in place and a qualified nurse visit Angel daily to administer medicine via the line.

Bill and Lily took Angel home on December 26, the day after Christmas. Lily sat down at her sewing machine and made a special sleeve for Angel's arm to hold the PICC line in place. But after sixteen days, the line became infected and had to be removed. As my mother put it, they couldn't treat one condition without aggravating another. From that point, they would have to treat her condition with oral medications and injections.

• • • •

Angel Rose had always loved the Christmas season. Lily and Bill would hang Christmas lights throughout the house, along with other colorful decorations. Included in the decorations were hundreds of cards from years gone by. There were cards from friends and family members, some of whom were long-since dead and gone. Angel loved the bright lights and the colors glistening in the reflection of the cards.

In thirty-four years, this was the first time Angel wasn't home for Christmas. Even though they kept the lights on long after the holidays, Angel didn't seem to notice them. They understood—they knew Angel would need time to heal. After all, it had taken several weeks for her to become as sick. It had taken several weeks just to diagnose the problem, during which time the infection grew even more inside Angel's body. Sepsis came closer to killing her than any sickness ever had.

After the long hospital stay of 2007, Lily and Bill watched Angel closely for signs that she was getting back to her happy and cheerful self, but it wasn't to be. Angel would never be the same. And more and more, they began to realize Angel was losing her sight. What could be more painful for a parent to endure, especially knowing how much Angel loved the sights and sounds of life?

The inability to see caused a dramatic change in Angel's behavior. She no longer enjoyed the outdoors. She now became frightened and confused when they took her outside. When they placed her in her swing, she would panic and reach out, as if she were afraid of falling. She also appeared to be suffering the effects of vertigo.

Angel didn't seem to enjoy life as much as she had before the loss of her sight. Her happy little world had gone dark.

And Jesus said to the blind man, "Go your way; your faith has made you well.
—MARK 10:52

Chapter Thirty-Nine

On the twenty-fourth day of February 2008, our mother turned eighty-four. And in the first hour of the twenty-sixth day of February, she passed away.

Up until 2000, our mother had been relatively healthy, considering she had been a cigarette smoker for forty-six years. In spite of repeated warnings from doctors, she continued to smoke. That all changed in August 2000, when she suffered a mild stroke. The stroke would prove to be a blessing in disguise. She recovered completely and never had a craving to smoke again.

Our mother was just a young girl when she became a mother. Having lots of children meant at least one thing: she would never be lonely. Except for Lily and me, her other children all lived close by.

She was just fifty-nine when our father passed away, and so she lived alone for the last twenty-five years of her life. The fact that she lived alone was not a reason for pity, for she kept herself well occupied.

She had a Citizens' Band radio known as a homebase unit, and she would talk for hours each night to friends and loved ones. Radio signal was somewhat limited in the mountains, but having her antenna placed high on the mountain gave her a signal reach of fifteen to twenty miles. She became quite popular with her CB buddies as "Momma Short Stuff." She truly loved her radio pals, and talking to them was one of her favorite pastimes. Our mother maintained her own radio equipment. For instance, if a tree branch fell on the line leading to the antenna, she would make the trip up the mountain to repair it.

She also kept a menagerie of animals around, especially chickens. She enjoyed the fresh eggs, but the sound of a farm was what she enjoyed the most. Charles and Jimmy were visiting her in the spring of 2004 when she complained about a fox preying on her young chickens. Jimmy said to her, "You know what you need, Mother? You need a barn." Nothing could have made her happier, so Charles and Jimmy built her a very nice two-stall barn complete with a hayloft.

The last thing I expected from my aging mother was her acquiring Sherman. Sherman was a talking bird. He was light green and stood about eight to ten inches tall. That bird would imitate every sound he heard. If two or more people were talking, he would command, "Be quiet!" His favorite toy was a set of keys on a ring. He would stand by the door on one foot, twirling the keys, and declare, "I'm leaving." He would ask for "Popesi" (Pepsi), and when he was given someone's almost empty can, he would lick the remaining drops, burp, and exclaim, "Cold beer." He would then make a loud ringing sound identical to the ringing of the phone and say, "Don't answer it."

Sherman also learned a few words he probably shouldn't have. For this, I would have to blame our youngest brother, Randy.

My mother also had a small dog, and the bird learned to imitate the dog. He would bark just like the dog. My mother used to say to him, "Sherman, honey, stop growling."

Sherman simply wandered about the house during the day, and at night he was told to "go home," and he would then climb into his cage. The cage was covered, and Sherman would

proclaim loudly, "Good night!" and then he would become completely silent.

For whatever reason, that bird hated our sister Rose. The
minute she came in, Sherman became agitated. He would immediately stop what he was doing and attempt to bite her.

• • • •

I've spent an incredible amount of time on the road working as a telecommunications contractor. Mid-November 2005
through February 2006, I helped repair communications lines
for BellSouth after Hurricane Wilma hit Miami, Florida. Mid-
December 2007 through mid-January 2008, I was in Tulsa,
Oklahoma, after a major ice storm. For six weeks following Tulsa,
I worked in Baxter Springs, Kansas.

I called my mother often when I was on the road. I prom-
ised her that as soon as the Kansas project was complete, I would
come visit her in Kentucky. On February 18, 2008, I finished
work in Kansas and went home to Minnesota. I had an extremely
busy season coming up in the spring, summer, and fall of that year,
and in order to keep up with the work, I would need more equipment. There was a good price on a piece of equipment out in
Portland, Oregon. However, it was first-come-first-served, and if
I didn't get out there with a cashier's check immediately, I would
miss the opportunity to buy it.

I knew our mother was in extremely poor health, but as I
had with Deanie, I thought there was more time. My plan was to
catch a flight to Oregon, buy the machine, put it on a rented truck,
and drive back to Minnesota. I could do it all in just a few days. I
would then fly out to Kentucky and spend a week with my mother.

I spoke with her on the phone on Saturday, February 23. She

was in the hospital, but she said they were planning to let her go home the next day, for her eighty-fourth birthday.

We booked a flight to Portland and left on February 23. We had a connecting flight in Denver and another at LAX in Los Angeles. But things didn't go well. We had to run to catch the plane in Denver and again at LAX. Then when we arrived in Portland, we had no luggage. The next day, I got up early and took the shuttle back to the airport to get our bags.

It was late in the afternoon when we were finally ready to leave Portland. With nearly two thousand miles to drive back to Minnesota, we were already running far behind schedule. I had plotted a route that would take us east through the Columbia River Gorge, north into eastern Washington, where we would get on Interstate 90 and back to Minnesota.

We were just on the outskirts of Portland when my cell phone rang. Lily said, "It's happening, Wynn," and she began to cry. "Our mother is dying."

I asked, "How long, Lily?" She told me her vital organs had begun to fail and the doctors were guessing two days to a week.

We stopped for the night in some small town in eastern Washington, and when there was no bad news by the next morning, I began to think I was going to get back in time. We stopped only for fuel and a quick meal in Spokane before driving all the way to Rocker, Montana. It was not an easy drive, however, on mountain roads, and snow was falling most of the way.

At about 2:00 a.m. Mountain Time on February 26, my cell phone rang. It was my sister-in-law Bonnie. She called to let me know our mother had just passed away.

Our mother had spent her final days at The King's Daughter hospital in Ashland. Some family members were at the hospital, and plans were in place for a birthday celebration. As of midafternoon on February 24, everyone thought she was about to be released from the hospital.

But then a doctor walked into the lobby where family members were waiting and announced some horrible and unexpected news. The doctor said, "Your mother is not going home. She's dying, and someone's going to have to tell her. I'm guessing she's got between two days and one week to live." The doctor then turned and walked away.

Charles accepted the painful task of telling our mother of her rapidly approaching death. I'm not sure how he was able to do it, but Charles sat down at her bedside and said, "The doctor just came out and talked to us. I'm afraid it's not good."

"What do you mean?" she asked.

Charles said, "The doctor says you're not going to make it this time."

Our mother, a person of great dignity, simply said, "Well, okay. Did he say how long?"

Charles said, "Maybe a week." He then asked, "Would you be more comfortable here at the hospital, or would you like to go home?"

She said, "I would like you to take me home."

They took our mother home to die. She lived through the night and until just after midnight on the twenty-sixth.

Our youngest brother, Randy, lived just across the creek from our mother's house. Randy simply couldn't bear to watch his mother die, and although there were a number of people watching over her, he remained home. At the hour of her death, Randy heard the sound of singing. The sound he heard was that of a choir singing more sweetly and clearly than anything he'd ever heard, but the sound seemed to be coming from above the roof of our mother's house. As is often customary in our religion, Randy thought church services were being held in the home.

The singing stopped, and Randy walked slowly back to Mother's house, where he found the crowd quiet and somber. After learning our mother had just passed away, he asked who had been singing. He was told there had been no singing—the people there had been completely quiet.

• • • •

Mother had her affairs in order. She had long since chosen her gravesite and had Lily make the dress she was to be buried in. She had also requested there be no viewing and the burial to be performed as quickly as possible. Therefore, I wasn't able to get to my mother's funeral in time. Family members offered to prolong the procedure to allow time for me to get there, but I didn't want to go against our mother's final wishes, so I told them to proceed without me. I did, however, make the trip to Weeksbury to spend some time with the family afterward.

I guess the hardest part was going into her home. There was a flowered dress lying on the guest bed that she was to wear home from the hospital. I could feel her presence throughout the house. I think Rose took her little dog, but then there was Sherman, her talking bird who had been so entertaining to her. Sherman sat, sad and somber, in his cage. He looked straight ahead, and in spite of efforts to get him to speak, Sherman remained silent, as if we weren't even there.

Her sorrows were known to man, her virtues were known to God.

—CHARLES DICKENS

Chapter Forty

It seemed the years were catching up with many people in both the Johnson and Skiles families. Johnny Ray Skiles is a typical member of the Skiles family: he's loving, caring, and always willing to help in any way he can. He's always been there with a positive and can-do attitude. Johnny gets his name from his dad. He's a few years older than Bill and has always been sensitive to Angel's condition.

Johnny Ray remembers the agony he and his wife, Barb, suffered when they lost their only son in 1970, as described in chapter 9. He always joins family members whenever there's a need. Lily remembers one of many wonderful things about Johnny Ray is that he would run out and bring back food for everyone. He made certain that if there were nothing else he could do, he would at least make sure everyone had something to eat. This is something so appreciated when it's not possible for loved ones to leave the bedside of a sick family member.

Johnny Ray worked at Springfield's International Harvester plant. One day in the early 1980s, he decided he was going to get himself into good physical condition. So instead of indulging in a long and relaxing lunch break, he began to jog. Each day, he'd jog a little farther and faster until a few yards became miles. Soon Johnny Ray was being called "The Marathon" by friends and coworkers.

He was a sportsman. Johnny Ray has spent many hours hunting and fishing. Today, however, he is in poor health, and sadly it's believed he's suffering from the same ailment that claimed the lives of his brothers Ronnie and Gerald. The most menial chores such as taking the garbage container to the curb for pickup are becoming too much for Johnny Ray. Doctors say the prognosis is grim and time is running out.

Eloise is becoming a victim of age as well. At eighty, she is now diabetic and no longer able to attend most family functions. This is excruciatingly painful for her. After all the years of being a driving force for the Skiles family, Eloise is forced to sit at home and wait for news, whether good or bad. The inability to come to Angel's bedside was extremely painful for her. When Angel's life began to slip away, Eloise could only sit at home, worry, wonder, and weep.

• • • •

There are a lot of health issues within our family, too. Linda, for instance, is now in poor health. She's now in her sixties, diabetic, and unable to walk. Perry is now seventy-three and suffers from congestive heart failure. For those of us unable to make the trip to see them, we stay in touch via the phone.

Rose, Lois, and Shirley have visited quite often. Lois is what I so lovingly call my "crazy sister." There's simply no way to feel down or depressed in her presence. She's truly a gift to our family. She's always happy with a joke to tell or something silly to say.

Jimmy's wife, Maggie, is an extraordinary lady as well. She has a somewhat quiet nature; however, everything she says is said with the fullest intention. Maggie is always there whenever she's needed. She's seen her share of sickness and death.

But understand this, that in the last days there will come times of stress.

—2 TIMOTHY 3:1

PART FIVE

Angel's Death

Chapter Forty-One

I've been a traveler for many years, and no matter where fate has taken me, I've always found the time to call Lily to ask about Angel's well-being. In the two years leading up to 2011, Lily had been telling me Angel's health was deteriorating. "Angel is just slipping away," she would say. Or, "I just know we're losing Angel."

Knowing at least part of her medical history and all the warnings from doctors that Angel had already beaten the odds, I was afraid she was right. In my heart, I didn't want to believe this, for what would the world be without Angel?

It began to worry me even more, when one day, I was having a conversation with my son, Jeremy, who lives within a mile or so of Lily and Bill. He said to me, "Dad, Uncle Bill and Aunt Lily are stressed to the breaking point. Bill's having a lot of trouble with his knees, and Lily is becoming frail. The three of them are not sleeping at all, and it's really starting to take its toll on them. You know, Dad, I'm not sure how they can go on. I'll tell you something else—they think Angel is now completely blind."

Throughout his life, Jeremy had always been extremely close to Lily, Bill, and Angel, and I could hear the sincere concern in his voice. This was the first mention to me of Angel's loss of eyesight. I immediately called Lily to ask her about it, and she told me the doctor said if Angel could see at all, then it was very little. The problem was the risk in sedating her in order to perform tests on her eyes. Doctors told Lily and Bill that if Angel were put to sleep, she would most likely never awaken.

So Lily searched the Internet for answers. The only practical solution was the Cleveland Clinic, where the ability to test people such as Angel existed. There was, however, a long waiting list. They contacted the clinic in early summer 2011, and the first opening was in mid-October. Once again, there was the painful waiting and the worry that perhaps October would be too late to save her sight. But there was no other choice but to wait—and hope for the best.

• • • •

Everything changed in late August 2011, when Angel developed a fever. Lily made an appointment with Dr. Venkatesh.

The doctor said, "Well, Lily, I'm not sure what else we can do without putting her to sleep for testing, and we know the risk involved in that. We're going to try her on cipro, a powerful antibiotic. You'll need to give it to her five days on and fourteen days off." The doctor continued, "In addition, I'm ordering blood work. There's a program called Outreach, and they'll come to your home to draw the blood samples."

Lily and Bill followed the doctor's instructions to the letter, but the fever remained. Another doctor's visit was arranged, and Dr. Venkatesh said, "It seems the cipro has stopped working. Now we're going to try doxy for the next five days, and that should take care of the problem."

Lily tried the new medication for the next five days, and again the fever seemed to become worse. Dr. Venkatesh next said, "Okay, Lily, we're going to try ampicillin." Again there was no improvement, so she recommended doxy for another five days.

On the evening of Wednesday, September 28, 2011, Angel's condition became severe. Dr. Venkatesh instructed them to take Angel to the emergency room at Springfield Regional Medical Center, which was the new name of the same Community Hospital Angel had been born in.

They put Angel into her wheelchair, and as they were leaving the house, she whispered, "Aite, aite, aite." This was Angel's way of saying, "I'm all right, I'm all right—please don't take me to the hospital." Somehow Angel knew a dark fate awaited her and she would never see home again. Angel's mind had developed to that of about a two-year-old's, yet in many ways, she was intelligent and mature. She had an uncanny way of knowing what was going to happen next.

They arrived with Angel late in the evening. Lily sat holding Angel's hand as a nurse pierced Angel's arm repeatedly but was unable to administer an IV. This is a painful procedure that usually caused Angel to cry. This time, however, she showed no resistance. Angel was just too weak and in too much pain.

The nurse finally said, "Mrs. Skiles, I'm not going to stick her anymore." The nurse was beside himself, and he was very apologetic he was unable to help Angel. He said, "Mrs. Skiles, Angel is going to need a PICC line, but there's no way it's going to be put into place tonight. So we'll have to do the best we can until the doctor comes in tomorrow."

Lily had a Tylenol and a bottle of milk in her bag. She crushed the Tylenol into a powder, mixed it with milk, and had Angel drink it. She asked Bill to return home for some other things she and Angel might need. Bill was only gone for a short time, and when he returned, Lily was still waiting for the hospital staff to prepare a bed for Angel. It was in the early hours of the twenty-ninth that Angel was finally put to bed. A long and sleepless night awaited Lily and Bill.

. . . .

Lily and Bill have always acknowledged the efforts and kindness of medical personnel. However, during Angel's final days in the hospital, they were appalled at the behavior of some of the staff. Lily and Bill were first surprised to learn Dr. Venkatesh had not been notified of Angel's condition, considering she was the one who instructed them to bring Angel to the emergency room. When they asked about calling Dr. Venkatesh, they were told she had absolutely no authority in that hospital.

Bill and Lily also didn't understand why the staff took Angel off the medication she had been taking since she was a child. When Lily asked why, a nurse told her, "We're going to do this our way. We know what we're doing."

Finally, they were confused about the catheter supposedly put into place to monitor Angel's urine output. A nurse came into the room in the early hours of the morning and asked, "When was the last time this bag was emptied?"

Lily replied, "It's never been emptied."

The nurse then said, "This was supposed to have been emptied every hour on the hour." The nurse simply took the bag to the toilet and dumped it, then walked away without saying another word. This led Lily and Bill to wonder why the catheter had been inserted if the urine was not being measured or tested.

I have to think the medical staff knew the work they were doing was futile; Angel, to them, was a lost cause. I'm sure they'd seen it all before. However, they also appeared to be underscoring what Lily and Bill had seen with Angel. For how many times had they been told Angel's condition was too severe and that she would not recover, and how many times had Lily and Bill proved them wrong? Lily and Bill would never give up until they knew Angel had taken her last breath.

As the medical staff prepared to insert the PICC line on Thursday morning, a nurse said to Lily and Bill, "Only one of you can be present for this procedure."

But Bill said, "No—we're both going to stay."

Seeing the extreme concern and worry, the staff made no other objection.

Lily and Bill knew the medication would take time to go into effect, so all they could do was wait, watch, and pray. The hours of Thursday slowly ticked by as Angel showed little or no signs of improvement.

They sat in the hospital room and occasionally watched the traffic as carefree people hurried passed the hospital. Something in their subconscious made Lily and Bill think, how dare these people go about their merry way, completely oblivious to the suffering within the walls of this building? How could those people's lives be so different, so simple, and so easy, as Bill and Lily had to watch their daughter fight for her life? They watched as the light of day faded, bringing on another agonizing night.

The only thing that kept them from collapsing was the hope that every passing moment would bring some improvement to Angel's condition. They kept thinking the medicine would begin to take effect, and they would all go home in a couple of days. They kept telling themselves they'd been through worse; they could make it if Angel could. After all, this wasn't the first time. Just a couple more days or even a week—they could hold on.

He gives power to the faint, and to him who has no might He increases strength.

—Isaiah 40:29

Chapter Forty-Two

On Friday morning, Angel was examined first by Dr. Jarvis, a kidney specialist, and then Dr. Hismogie, who specializes in the treatment of infections. Both doctors concurred that with the direct application of antibiotics via the PICC line, the medicine would soon begin to take effect, and Angel would be going home after about two days.

I was in a somewhat remote region of southeast Minnesota when I noticed I had missed a call from my son. I thought I would wait until I was in an area with better cell phone reception before returning his call. I was away from the phone for a few moments when I noticed he had called again. This time, I thought I had better listen to his message. He said, "Dad, I left you a message earlier that Angel's vital organs were beginning to fail. I want you to disregard that message. It seems someone made a mistake. I think Angel's going to be okay."

Jeremy gave me the hospital room number, and when I called, Bill answered. I asked how she was, and Bill said, "Well, they've got this PICC line in her again, and if it works as well as it did before, then she'll be okay. The doctors said she might get to go home in a couple of days."

But something in Bill's voice told me he was very worried. At first I thought it was sheer exhaustion, but there was much more than that. Bill and Lily knew Angel Rose more than anyone. They knew every sign, every symptom, and they recognized even the slightest change in her. They often knew exactly what to expect long before the doctors, for they had seen it all at least once before.

• • • •

But then one of the on-call staff doctors came in to examine Angel. Bill said to her, "Dr. Jarvis and Dr. Hismogie said we should be able to take Angel home in a couple of days. Do you agree?"

The doctor said, "No—apparently the doctors haven't looked at the charts. I don't think she'll be going home."

Unable to speak, Lily and Bill sank slowly into chairs. The doctor then left the room.

I understand doctors are subjected to pain and suffering on a daily basis, and bedside manner is not always their top priority. However, this was Bill and Lily's life—without Angel, there was nothing left for them.

Jeremy had stayed close to Lily and Bill at the hospital. Lily and Bill were too grief stricken to fully understand everything as it was happening. When the doctor came around, Jeremy spoke with her. It seemed the fears I had heard earlier were true. Despite the earlier prognosis, the doctor now confirmed Angel appeared to be slipping away.

As they waited for a change in her condition, the hospital staff remained skeptical. It was as if Bill and Lily were the only two people in the world who cared whether Angel lived or died. Could this be the case, or did the staff know something they didn't? How could the hospital staff be so doubtful? Lily and Bill literally watched the medicine flow into Angel's body. How could it be ineffective? Where was this medicine going, if it wasn't fighting the infection in her body? They thought, where there was life, there was hope. The PICC line was still in place, pumping powerful drugs into Angel's body nonstop around the clock.

• • • •

Other family members began to arrive in support of Angel. Bill's brother Johnny Ray was ever present, and as usual, he was willing to do anything to help. Eloise was unable to go to the hospital, but other supporters began to arrive. Friends, family members, and members of the church visited.

As the treatment continued without improvement, the people around them became more and more concerned, but Lily and Bill were completely undaunted. As long as Angel was alive, they clung to the notion that they would be taking her home in a couple of days.

Ernie and his wife, Judy, made the trip from Kentucky. They arrived late on Friday afternoon. Jeremy met them at Lily and Bill's house and drove them to the hospital. Angel had lots of uncles, but she had her favorites. When Ernie walked into the hospital room, Angel perked up immediately. Ernie kept telling her he was going to steal her "ming-ming" or her milkshake. Angel smiled, pulled him down, and kissed his cheek. They stayed at the hospital until late in the evening and then had Jeremy drive them back to Lily's to rest for a short while before returning to the hospital.

Having heard a grim view of Angel's health from Jeremy, I called Ernie, perhaps in search of better news. Ernie and Judy are strong and devout Christians. Ernie had a different opinion all together. He didn't seem sad or worried; he was actually cheerful and uplifting. He said, "Wynn, I have word from a higher authority that Angel will be coming out of that hospital tomorrow afternoon."

For a moment, I thought he was referring to a new prognosis from a doctor, and my spirits began to rise. But then I realized this message he was speaking of was spiritual. Yet he seemed so confident—somehow he just knew Angel was going to be leaving the hospital on Saturday afternoon. With that message in mind, plus everything else I had heard, I continued to worry.

Like everyone else, Jeremy was still convinced Angel would be going home soon. When Angel's condition seemed to get worse, Jeremy stayed at the hospital unless he was asked to run an errand.

When I asked Jeremy to give an account of the events of Angel's final hours, he said, "Dad, nothing matched, nothing made sense, and nothing seemed to be real. We had a doctor and nurses telling us Angel was dying, and we had doctors telling us she would be going home soon. We all chose to believe the latter. You know how it is when you're sad, depressed, and desperate. It was weird—the whole world looked physically different. It's hard to explain."

For God speaks in one way, and in two, though man does not perceive it.

—Job 33:14

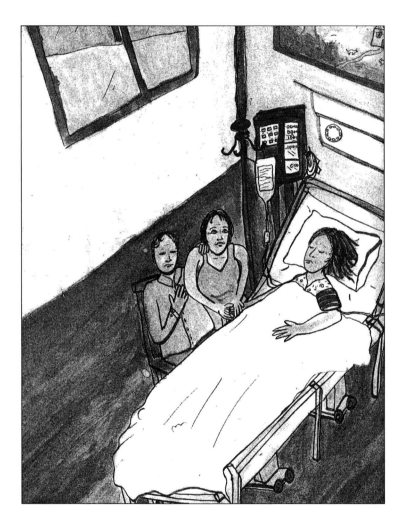

Chapter Forty-Three

Autumn comes early in the Upper Midwest. There was a slight chill in the air on October 1, 2011, a definite reminder that summer was gone. The sun on my sweatshirt was much-needed warmth as I prepared for a day of work in western Minnesota in the Wheaton–Herman area. I left the Twin Cities early in order to link up with a coworker by midmorning. It was an incredibly bright and cloudless day. Passing the local farm markets along the way was a reminder of my intention to pick up some pumpkins and a bundle of corn to decorate the front yard for the autumn season.

I was trying not to think about Angel Rose. I was so absolutely sure Lily and Bill would pull her through, just as they had all the times before. I comforted myself with the notion that Angel had been much sicker than this before and still beat the odds. Angel would never let this get her down.

I was wrong.

The following pages give an account of by far the saddest and most painful event I have ever had to endure.

• • • •

Throughout the day on Friday, Lily and Bill were lost in some dark oblivion. Until the moment when the staff doctor told them Angel was dying, Bill and Lily had been watching for signs of improvement and something to reassure them they could all go home soon and get some rest. Now they hung on to what the other two doctors had said as one last sliver of hope. After all, this other doctor wasn't the first to say Angel's time had come. They thought, "How did she know? She wasn't even Angel's doctor. What would Dr. Venkatesh have to say, if she were here?" They were simply not going to listen to anyone who said Angel wouldn't be going home. They would wait for the other two doctors and hope the rest of the staff would stay away from Angel's bedside.

How can it be that time could pass so slowly? Were they the only people in the world to suffer such agony? There were sounds throughout the hospital, but to Lily, Bill, and Angel, the day went unnoticed. The cleaning, the changing of the beds, the occasional giggling of the hospital staff, nothing caught their attention. Their lives and their world and their future lay before them sweet and dying.

Deep inside, perhaps they knew this could be Angel's time, for in her darkest hours, they had never experienced these feelings. This was somehow different from all the other near misses with Angel. Even without that doctor predicting Angel's passing, the feeling would still be different. It was as if some hidden defenses were beginning to build inside them, preparing them for what was to happen next. There was some invisible and divine presence in that room, something unexplainable they never before experienced.

As time passed, they became more and more aware that what was happening was unstoppable and unchangeable. Their future was being altered and reshaped with every passing second. They were aware that no matter how much they prayed or how much they pleaded, Angel's fate was at hand.

Completely unable to focus, they held Angel's hand, they openly wept, and they prayed aloud. In separate visions, they revisited every moment of Angel's life over and over in their minds. Through the torturous hours, they waited and longed to see Dr. Jarvis or Dr. Hismogie. These were the two men who had given them hope. Perhaps by the time they arrive in the morning, they thought, Angel's condition would have improved.

• • • •

Angel was restless and obviously in pain during the night on Friday, September 30, and into Saturday, October 1. Again, the only thing they could do was hold her hand and wait. Through the long night, they watched as Angel's head turned from side to side. At one point, she asked for "wa-wa," so they asked if she could have some water. The doctor said only they as parents were permitted to give her water, but she advised they not give her any. Lily put a few drops of water on some paper towels and moistened her lips.

In the early morning hours of Saturday, a nurse rushed into the room and asked if Angel had made any sudden moves or perhaps had a coughing episode. Bill said no and then asked why. The nurse said the monitor indicated a spike in Angel's heart rate. The nurse went on to say this was usually followed by death.

Once again, their hope sank even deeper into despair. They kept thinking it had to be the absolute worst of bad dreams. There's just no way fate could be so cruel as to take everything at once. But Lily also kept thinking about a favor she had asked of God. She had asked God to take Angel before she and Bill became unable to care for her. They had both seen their health beginning to decline, and they just couldn't think about the fate that would befall Angel in their absence. There was no friend or relative with the skill or equipment to care for her.

They put their faith in the wisdom of God.

About 6:00 a.m. Angel indicated she would like to play, so they pulled the serving table over to her bed and placed one of her favorite toys in front of her. For a few minutes, she tried to play, but then her hands fell limp at her sides.

At 6:30, their hopes lifted once again when Dr. Jarvis, the kidney specialist, came in. After examining Angel, the doctor said, "Angel is very weak, and if she pulls through, we're going to need to invade the kidney from the back. We will then enter the bladder to examine a mass that we think could be cancer. She's also going to need hospice care and dialysis."

Lily asked, "Is this something that would take place in a nursing home or here at the hospital?"

The doctor began to reply, explaining that it depended on her response to the treatment. But at that moment, an extraordinary event occurred. Lily was the only person in the room to witness it. It did, however, take place, just as sure as the sunrise of the morning. Perhaps it was Lily's fatigue or her closeness to Angel, but for whatever the reason, this event was meant for her only.

As the doctor was speaking, there was an interruption in the sound of his words. It was as if someone had turned down the volume on the doctor's voice and Lily could not hear it. There was, without a shadow of a doubt, another presence within the room. An invisible, physical manifestation of a spirit. The spirit was opposed to everything the doctor was saying. It was as if the spirit was saying, "No, you will not cut this child, for I am taking her."

As the doctor left the room, Lily had a feeling of great peace and understanding, for now she knew God's plan. She knew Angel was being taken to a place of health and happiness. She knew now Angel was going to be okay. She had never worried about Angel's spiritual well-being, but the holy being who visited the hospital room was a confirmation of their faith.

Angel pulled Momma down and gave her a night-night kiss. About ten minutes later, she took three short, rapid breaths, looked straight ahead, closed her eyes, and was gone. Johnny Ray ran into the hallway, screaming for help. The doctor came in and confirmed she had passed.

Angela Rose Skiles passed away at 6:50 a.m. on October 1, 2011.

Jeremy arrived about seven minutes later to find Lily and Bill still holding her hand and sobbing inconsolably. Johnny Ray stood staring straight ahead as if he were unable to speak.

A nurse walked into the room and said, "I told you this was going to happen." It was nothing short of cruel. It was as if she were gloating in the fact her prediction had been correct, as if Lily and Bill shouldn't be weeping for their daughter because if they had listened to the nurse, they would have been more prepared for her death.

• • • •

Shortly after Angel passed away, Lily and Ernie were standing by her bed when Lily had another extraordinary experience. Angel's body had been covered with her favorite blanket. As Lily stood dazed, looking at her body, something supernatural began to take place.

Slowly, an image began to appear on Angel's abdomen. It was the shape of a large pencil, and it was a brilliant emerald-green. The image seemed to be moving and somewhat translucent. Then the image began to split at the point. One part of the image pointed toward Angel's head, and the other part pointed to her feet. Lily then heard an unexplainable voice, sweeter and clearer than she had ever heard. The voice said, "*You are now separated.*" Lily said to Ernie, "Are you seeing this, Ernie? Did you hear that voice?"

Ernie said, "No, Lily, I didn't see or hear anything."

As Lily continued to watch, the image began to fade, and in its place, another image appeared. Lily described it as looking at moon craters. Some of the craters were small, but one larger crater formed in the center and appeared to be bottomless. Lily cried out, "I can see where Angel is going, and I don't like it."

Through these moments following Angel's death, the spiritual presence within the room was unexplainably stronger than ever. It was enough to sway the belief of any nonbeliever and strong enough to reinforce the faith of believers. There was the undeniable presence of death, but also a glimpse of a new beginning for Angel Rose. She wasn't forever gone from life, but simply moving to a new location and starting a new life.

Some people present at the time felt a strange presence, but nothing to compare with what Lily and Bill experienced. I have to think it was supposed to be this way. What they saw and felt was meant only for them. I think most friends and relatives who were present thought Lily was having an illusion, perhaps brought on by fatigue and sleep deprivation. But a month or so after this event, Lily saw a show on the Discovery Channel that featured the accounts of people who were clinically dead for a short time and then resuscitated. Each and every one of these people described visions similar to or exactly the same as what Lily had seen on Angel's body. In order to get to the afterlife, each person has to pass through what appears to be a tunnel.

I'm sure skeptics would pass this whole thing off as illusion. One thing is certain, and that is I've never known Lily to be untrue about anything. I truly believe what she saw was as real as the sunrise in the morning. I know the closeness of the physical bond between Lily and her daughter, and to people of faith, there is no such thing as skepticism.

• • • •

Lily continued holding Angel's hand for the next two hours. As her body became cold, Angel's hand slowly closed around Lily's. The hospital chaplain came in to offer sustenance as Lily and Bill were joined by numerous friends and relatives. There were members of the Johnson and the Skiles families. There were also members of Bill and Lily's church. It was only the pleadings of these friends and family members that finally convinced Lily and Bill to let go so Angel's body could be taken care of.

But go your way till the end; and you shall rest, and shall stand in your allotted place at the end of days.
—DANIEL 12:13

Chapter Forty-Four

The next day, Lily and Bill somehow found the strength to make the funeral arrangements. They were joined by a large group of supporters, and this, I believe, was the only way they were able to get through it. Lily chose a coffin, and she had Angel dressed in her pink pajamas Momma had made for her. They had her blanket she so loved placed in the coffin, with her fingers inserted through the holes, as this was the way Angel slept. Finally, they placed her favorite toy, Woo-Woo, in with her as well. It was just as if Lily and Bill were putting Angel to bed.

They couldn't bear the thought of placing Angel's body in the ground, so with the trust fund they had set up for her years before, they purchased a mausoleum. Angel's remains were to be kept clean and dry for eternity. There is a place for the three of them in the mausoleum.

On October 4, 2011, Angela Rose Skiles was entombed at Ferncliff Cemetery of Springfield. Ferncliff is a beautiful cemetery that borders a large city park called Snyder Park. A rather large stream flows between the cemetery and the park. Angel loved that park, and it seems only fitting her tomb overlooks the stream and a small waterfall.

The temperature that day was perfect, and the deep blue autumn sky was cloudless. As they drove the winding lanes of the cemetery, Lily watched as an occasional maple or sycamore leaf floated gently to the soft green grass. How could they possibly find the willpower to leave Angel on such a perfect day? There had been so many days just like this one when they would go for a drive in the country for hours and then end the day with a milkshake or ice cream. Is it possible all they had enjoyed in life was now gone?

As the funeral service ended, friends and family members began to scatter to the winds. They hadn't seen or heard from some people at Angel's funeral in years, and as they departed, Lily and Bill had a strange feeling they would probably never see them again. They felt that if it took such a tragedy to bring them together, then the next catastrophe might be one of their own funerals. As they watched their friends and family leave the cemetery, they began to feel the loneliness of the woeful future that awaited them.

• • • •

As it usually happens, the visitors began to visit less frequently, and the phone stopped ringing as often. After a month, Bill had to return to work, leaving home at 2:30 p.m. and returning at about midnight. Work was therapeutic for Bill; he made every effort to develop a new routine and new habits. As he told me not long after Angel's passing, "It's a little easier for me because I've always had at least nine hours at work each day all these years, while Lily was with her twenty-four hours a day and seven days a week."

In the months after Angel passed away, I talked to Lily on a daily basis, and there was not one time when she didn't break down and sob. It's impossible to measure the amount of suffering they were forced to endure. I was trying, as I'm sure all the family was trying, to convince Lily and Bill things would get better. They were fully aware Angel has gone on to await them in another world. But this is little comfort for parents who loved their child as much as they loved Angel. Their happy home on Sudbury Street, once teeming with all the cheerful sounds of Angel's presence, was now deathly quiet.

Lily said her life ended on that day in October. There was no use in trying to go on. All was lost. Bill told me they had always imagined and hoped that when Angel died, they'd live only long enough to see her put away to their wishes, and then they would join her within just a few days.

The only thing I could say was, "Bill, I'm sure you know fate is often cruel and unfair. You also know that we all love you, and we'd like to keep the two of you around for a long time. After all, time has no measurements in Angel's new world. And if you live for another hundred years, it's only a blink of an eye in her world. When your time comes, you'll find her just as she was, only free of pain and sickness."

I didn't need to remind Bill of those things. I think I was reassuring myself as much as anything. Even with this knowledge, there was no relief for the longing to see their darling child, to touch her, and to hold her. They still yearned to put her into her bed each night and know she was safe and warm. How could they come to terms with the fact that everything they had ever lived for was gone? It seemed so unreal that their daughter is in some box in a mausoleum, cold and alone.

• • • •

After her passing, Lily and Bill returned to the restaurants they used to visit with Angel. Whenever the staff would see them in the drive-through lane, they'd have Angel's shake made to order, just the way she liked it. The entire staff would then come to the window to wave and say hello to Angel. But now the window opened, and the girl said, "One shake with whipped cream." Bill responded sadly, "No, we won't need the shakes anymore."

Lily and Bill also visited all of Angel's favorite Walmart stores with the sad news she had died. There were lots of sad faces and many tear-filled eyes among the staff, as if a part of their day was now gone.

Whoever humbles himself like this child, he is the greatest in the kingdom of heaven.

—Matthew 18:4

Chapter Forty-Five

For months, I tried to convince Lily something would happen to ease their pain. I had no idea what it would be, but I somehow believed fate would loosen its death grip on them. I wasn't just saying this to give her a false sense of hope; I sincerely believed it.

However, in the dead of winter, not too many things change, so I kept telling her, "Lily, let's take one day at a time. Each day moves us a little closer to spring. You can start your flower garden then, you can travel to Kentucky, and more than anything, you and Bill can visit me in Minnesota. There is so much I've always wanted to show you here, including the North Shore of Lake Superior."

"You don't understand," she said to me. "All means nothing to me now."

I tried to convince her to start driving again. "Just take a short trip around the block, or visit Jeremy. He's just a mile from your house."

"No way," she said. "I'm just too distraught. I'm afraid I might hurt someone."

Still, I remained confident some unexpected event would turn things around for them. It began with a visit to Weeksbury during the holidays. Lily was reminiscing with my brother Charles about being a little girl and living in the old house that sat on a hill. I can vaguely remember the old house, but I was just a little kid when it was torn down. To my older brothers and sisters, it was their childhood home.

She said, "You know, Charles, I can remember a lot of happy times up on that hill. You can see the entire hollow from up there. Mother used to have the most beautiful gardens up there. I've often dreamed of sitting on the front porch and looking at the moonlight on that mountain on the other side. That was a peaceful place to live and one I'll never forget."

Charles pondered for a moment and then said, "Lily, that doesn't have to be just a dream. You own a mobile home—we have equipment. We'll build a road and move it up there. We'll put it in the same spot where the old house used to be, complete with the front porch. Then you can have your flower garden, your vegetable garden, or whatever you like."

At first, such a large task seemed to be completely insurmountable to Lily. She was, to say the least, skeptical it could be done. But to Charles and Jimmy, who've spent their entire adult lives running heavy equipment, it was no great feat.

For the first time since Angel died, Lily had found a purpose and a reason to live. It's going to be a challenge for her and Bill when spring arrives in 2012. There'll be raking, seeding, and all kinds of landscaping to do. This is probably just what they needed, but spring seems so far away—and would it mean anything without Angel?

Within a couple of days, the project got underway. Ernie removed the skirting and the porch, while Charles and Jimmy placed a culvert to cross the creek and built the driveway. This kind of work can be a challenge during the winter months. Rain often falls for days on end, but by the first week in February, they had home in place.

Another wonderful thing happened during that trip. Family members chipped in and purchased a tiny puppy for Lily. At first, they were very reluctant. Bill especially didn't want another pet; they still remembered the pain of losing Fluffy. To add to that, they didn't think they could love and care for the dog in their present state of mind.

But they didn't have to love the dog, for the dog loved them. Lily described the dog as tiny as a teacup. They took the little dog for a one-night trial. Lily said the puppy slept in her hair that night. They named her Kandy, and the bond was unbreakable. Lily pampers Kandy. She wraps her in a blanket and rocks her to sleep. Kandy follows them like a shadow.

Lily and Bill are far from recovery, but thanks to some well-wishing and thoughtful relatives who love them very much, it's a start. Even though Lily says the pain is still as fresh as ever, I think there might be a little improvement. Kandy helps keep Lily and Bill occupied during these long and cold winter months, and when Lily cries, Kandy cries as well. Tears form in her little eyes, and she genuinely begins to weep.

Two months ago, you would have thought there was no hope for Lily. So much of her was gone. I didn't think she would ever feel another happy thought. But now I truly believe there's hope.

• • • •

The contract between the union and the management at Robbins & Myers has reached its three-year duration. The company is now operating on a day-to-day basis until terms are agreed upon and a new three-year contract is in place. The company is attempting to reduce employee wages and other benefits, and they are completely unwilling to compromise. Some employees believe the company is trying to break the union. Bill says if this happens, he will put in for retirement.

I don't think anything could please me more than seeing Bill retire. I've never known any family who's worked so hard, who's struggled to get what they have, and then who's had to fight so hard to hang onto it. It's time for them to rest now and at least try to enjoy the remainder of their lives together. A lifetime of toil is coming to a painful end for them. There are still a lot of family members to be with, as well as some new experiences I would like to see them try.

Forgetting what lies behind and straining forward to what lies ahead.

—PHILIPPIANS 3:13

Chapter Forty-Six

Bill and Lily have always become somewhat offended when someone suggested Angel might have been a burden to them. Lily says,
"Angel was no burden. I enjoyed every minute of her life, and I
would cherish the opportunity to do it all again."

About ten days after Angel died, Lily had the dream again.
Now the child is waiting for her.

God himself will be with them; he will wipe away every tear
from their eyes, and death shall be no more, neither shall
there be mourning nor crying nor pain any more, for the
former things have passed away.

—REVELATIONS 21:4

EPILOGUE

We've suffered the loss of several close friends and family members since Angel passed away. Life flows smoothly for long periods of time, and then it seems as if death is all around you. Most notably was the loss of our sister Linda. As mentioned, Linda had for some time lived in poor health. On May 11, 2012, she suffered a stroke. When she learned she would be forever bedfast and without sight, she asked that all medical assistance be removed. This was after her skull was uncapped to relieve pressure and swelling of the brain. Linda was a devout Christian who had worked hard to earn her reward in heaven, and she was ready to go and claim it. Even without medical assistance, she lived in agony until six weeks from the day of her stroke she died on the twenty-second day of June.

Johnny Ray Skiles was Bill's brother who was named in honor of their father, John Skiles. John was one of Angel's favorite uncles. He was ever present whenever Angel became sick. Again as mentioned, John was in the room when Angel passed away. John, who was a distance runner only twenty-five years ago, developed a rare and incurable lung disease, just like his brothers Gerald and Ronny. He died on October 22, 2012.

And we wait in our turn to disappear like snow before the summer sun.
—TECUMSEH OF THE SHAWNEE, 1794

ACKNOWLEDGMENTS

Where to begin . . .

First I'll say thank you to my sweetheart, Jessica, for her help and understanding.

To my beloved brother and lifelong companion, Charles— even when the miles between us numbered in the thousands, we kept in touch. Charles has always been gifted with an excellent knack for remembering things. His unique gift of memory was a great source for true events that had been long-since brushed from my mind. Other family members played a large part in helping me to recall certain events as well.

I would like to thank Amy Quale from Beaver's Pond Press for the motivational kick in the pants. You got me going again, Amy.

Then there's Jamie Fischer, longtime friend and coworker. I feel the need to describe Jamie to you: take the tenacity of Helen Keller, the zeal of Margaret Thatcher, and the spirit of Sally Ride, then place it in a beautiful person, and you have Jamie. Jamie, whom I call James, has a tremendous amount of skill and knowledge. When my own insecurities were holding me back on this project, she was nothing short of forceful. She's a wonderful person and a good friend, but her nature remains a mystery to me.

It's a little strange and ironic that the person appointed to edit this book is named Angela. Angela Wiechmann received her bachelor's degree with honors from the University of Minnesota. Angie was the first to tell me my book was worth the effort, and for that, I'm eternally grateful. Angela's intelligence is far beyond my abilities; but Angie, you and I both know that without your touch of genius, this book would not be worth reading. Angie, you are truly a genius.

I'd like to say thanks to Jessica Danielzuk for the beautiful illustrations. A special thank you to my niece in Weeksbury, Savannah Johnson, for the Christmas scene on page 62.

I thank you, Lily and Bill, for your story and for all you mean to me. We're all older now, and each other is all we have.

And to Angel Rose, I thank you for your precious life. We miss you, honey. Oh, how we miss you.

ABOUT THE AUTHOR

My name is Wynn Johnson. I was born on June 28, 1954, in a small hospital in Virgie, Kentucky. Today, locals would argue there is no hospital in Virgie. That's because shortly after I was born, the wooden structure burned to the ground and was never rebuilt.

I spent the first seventeen years of my life growing up in the east Kentucky coal fields. I'm fairly certain that had I stayed there, I could have been happy and could have probably made a modest living. The problem with that, though, was my nagging spirit for adventure. And that's what life has been for me—a grand and glorious adventure.

On Friday April 15, 1968, my brothers Charles and Jimmy and I were camping at our favorite campsite atop Collier Rocks. As we lay on our blanket rolls, looking up into a cloudless night and a full moon, we talked about the future and what we would be when we grew up.

I remember saying, "You know, I think I'm going to be seeing that old moon from a lot of different angles in the world."

Charles then said, "No, I don't think so, Wynn. You'll probably be right here with the rest of us."

Well, fate had another plan in mind for me, for I have traveled to many places and seen many different cultures and ways of life. Of the things I treasure most are the memories of the many wonderful people I've met along the way.

My ability to tell stories comes from a life of travel and my passion for books. I have read many books, and I guess my love for reading was developed while serving as a marine at sea with the navy. When you've seen nothing but water for weeks on end, a Louis L'Amour novel describing a slow-running brook lined with cottonwood trees, a ranch house, and cattle grazing in green pastures paints a welcome picture in one's mind.

I happen to believe the answer to any question or the solution to any problem is written somewhere on the pages of a book. There are two problems that if eliminated would no doubt solve the problems of the entire world, and those two things are hunger and illiteracy.

However, this is not a book about me. It is a book about a lot of special and wonderful people, and I hope you enjoyed it.